Verbal Protocols of Reading:
The Nature of Constructively
Responsive Reading

Verbal Protocols of Reading: The Nature of Constructively Responsive Reading

Michael Pressley
University at Albany, State University of New York

Peter Afflerbach
University of Maryland at College Park

LEA LAWRENCE ERLBAUM ASSOCIATES, PUBLISHERS

1995 Hillsdale, New Jersey   Hove, UK

Lawrence Erlbaum Associates, Inc., Publishers
365 Broadway
Hillsdale, New Jersey 07642

Library of Congress Cataloging-in-Publication Data

Pressley, Michael.
    Verbal protocols of reading : the nature of constructively
responsive reading / Michael Pressley, Peter Afflerbach.
        p.   cm.
    Includes bibliographical references and indexes.
    ISBN 0-8058-1537-6. — ISBN 0-8058-1764-6 (pbk.)
    1. Reading, Psychology of.   2. Cognition—Research—Methodology.
I. Afflerbach, Peter.   II. Title.
BF456.R2P76   1995
418'.4'019—dc20   94-31355
                                                                  CIP

Books published by Lawrence Erlbaum Associates are printed on acid-free
paper, and their bindings are chosen for strength and durability.

Printed in the United States of America
10 9 8 7 6 5 4 3 2 1

Dedicated to the theorists whose work influenced
and guided ours, and to the practitioners whose work
in the teaching and learning of reading helps children
mature into constructively responsive readers.

This book is also dedicated to
James "Jacques" Afflerbach.

Contents

Preface

In the fall of 1989 Michael Pressley moved to the University of Maryland at College Park. For a variety of reasons, including a new friendship with John Guthrie, Pressley found himself thinking about reading comprehension in 1989–1990. That year, Peter Afflerbach interviewed successfully for a position in reading education at Maryland, joining the faculty in autumn, 1990. We became close friends, talking a great deal about reading in 1990–1991 and 1991–1992, working on projects such as the grant that in 1992 would fund the National Reading Research Center at the Universities of Maryland and Georgia. Because Pressley chose to conduct studies involving verbal protocols of reading, there was especially high incentive for interaction, for Afflerbach had conducted several such investigations in his career. It was decided in the spring of 1992 that we had made enough progress conceptually in our discussions of protocol analysis that it would make sense to attempt to conduct a session at the December 1992 meeting of the National Reading Conference on the methodology. Although a proposal for an NRC session was crafted in the spring of 1992, one which was accepted, neither author really knew what we would present in such a session, confident we could get our thoughts together by autumn. Fortunately, we did, enough to present a preliminary version of what is now chapter 3 of this volume. The audience reception was so positive that we knew we had to refine our thoughts and write this book, if for no other reason than to fulfill a desire by many reading researchers to know just what claims about reading are justified on the basis of existing protocols of reading.

The following spring we proposed to Hollis Heimbouch of Lawrence Erlbaum Associates, Inc., that we prepare a book on verbal protocol analysis. During a long luncheon with Hollis at the meeting of the American Educational Research Association in Atlanta, we committed to such a project, agreeing to deliver in the spring of 1994. Consistent with that promise, this preface is being drafted on the first day of spring, 1994, following a year of analysis and reanalysis of the verbal protocol data and many reflections on their significance.

We owe thanks to many people who assisted us in this work. Without Pamela El-Dinary (now at Georgetown University) and David Wyatt (now at Trinity College), Pressley would have never figured out how to analyze protocol data in order to illuminate the many processes in them: during 1989–1990, El-Dinary, Wyatt, and Pressley struggled long and hard to invent a coding scheme that would capture the reading of domain experts processing texts in their areas of expertise. Without the success of that effort, resulting in Wyatt et al. (1993), this book would have never happened. That effort was successful largely because Pamela, David, and Mike persevered until they came up with an analysis that was the very best they could possibly invent, an analysis that seems additionally credible in light of the outcomes reported in this book.

Since publishing a review of reading and verbal reporting in 1984, Afflerbach has continued helpful discussions on the nature of reading and literacy with Peter Johnston. Similarly, Afflerbach continues to benefit from the many conversations with undergraduate and graduate students and colleagues in the Department of Curriculum and Instruction at the University of Maryland. Afflerbach serves on the English/Language Arts Advisory Committee of the New Standards Project headed by David Pearson and Miles Myers. The experiences of interacting with the committee members helped in shaping the contribution to this book, through discussions about reading in its constructive and responsive aspects.

We appreciate deeply the warm reception to preliminary versions of this work from National Reading Conference colleagues, both at the 1992 session and at a follow-up workshop in 1993. Linda Kucan of the University of Pittsburgh deserves a special thanks for reading a preliminary draft and providing some important comments about how the case we make for constructively responsive reading could be strengthened. So does Joel Meyers of the University at Albany, who read chapter 4 and provided remarks stimulating us to expand our discussion of constructive responsivity. In 1993–1994, Allan Purves of the University at Albany talked with Michael Pressley about the project several times in hallway conversations. Although those meetings were brief, they came at points in the project when Pressley needed energizing. Both authors appreciate greatly the support of our National Reading Research Center colleagues, including John Guthrie, Linda Gambrell, Pat Koskinen, John O'Flahavan, and Bruce Van Sledright.

Our families deserve thanks as well. When the project was going well, they saw less of us than we would have liked; when it was going badly, we weren't as pleasant to have around as we should have been. Donna and Wendy were patient through it all. Tim Pressley was fascinated that Daddy was learning about reading, just as he was learning to read at school.

1

▼▼▼▼▼▼▼

An Introduction to Protocol Analysis of Reading

The understanding of human thoughts and actions continues as a goal of psychology and affiliated areas of inquiry. We begin this book by considering briefly the development of protocol analysis as a methodology for examining thought and action, the uses of protocol analysis in investigations of reading past and present, and the historic and ongoing concerns with verbal reports as data. The use of protocol analysis in reading is accompanied by a history of claims for and challenges to the methodology. This is a healthy situation, for the ongoing use of think-aloud protocols has provided information that can be used to refine the methodology. For some, the fact that protocol analysis is regularly used in the investigation of reading appears to be equated with the idea that it is a mature methodology. We consider protocol analysis to be a maturing methodology with much interesting work already accomplished and considerable work to be done.

In think-aloud studies, subjects report their thinking as they do a task. The use of think-aloud data in reading has occurred throughout the 20th century (e.g., Marbe, 1901; McCallister, 1930; Olshavsky, 1976–1977; Piekarz, 1954; Strang, 1970; Titchener, 1912a, 1912b), which is not surprising, because it has been used for thousands of years to reveal thinking. For example, Aristotle and Plato encouraged people to talk about what was on their minds (Boring, 1953; cited in Pritchard, 1990b). More recently, James (1890) used subjects' reports of their thinking to develop psychological theory. The use of protocol analysis in the 20th century has been used to reveal processing of diverse tasks, including physics problem solving (Simon & Simon, 1978), student cognitions during instruction Peterson, Swing, Braverman, & Buss, 1982), and reading comprehension (Olshavsky, 1976–1977).

Investigations of reading have used protocol analysis both as an exploratory methodology (i.e., inductively) and as a means of testing hypotheses about reading that emanate from initial explorations (i.e., deductively). Protocol analysis of reading has served a varied set of research agendas, including investigations of readers using context to derive word meanings (Werner & Kaplan, 1950), reasoning to complete cloze sentences (Bridge & Winograd, 1982), answering comprehension questions (Kavale & Schreiner, 1979), summarizing texts (Brown & Day, 1983), and reacting to texts in a field of expertise (Wineberg, 1991).

Huey (1908) suggested that the human achievement of reading has few if any equals. Using protocol analysis data related to reading, we make the case that Huey was right. We develop a rich description and understanding of cognitive and affective processes during reading. In doing so, we come to the conclusion that reading is *constructively responsive*—that is, good readers are always changing their processing in response to the text they are reading. The result is complex processing. The elegant description of reading that emerges from protocol analysis is proof enough of the utility of the method, although throughout this book we attempt to increase awareness of the limitations of protocol analysis, although our perspective is that the limitations in no way diminish the promise of protocol analysis. The results summarized in this volume are only a beginning, for we believe a much more detailed understanding of reading can be developed through future, more analytical uses of protocol analysis.

CHALLENGES TO PROTOCOL ANALYSIS

Whatever the value of people's reports of their thinking, there are important challenges to the validity of protocol analysis. Protocol analysis is all about the relation of peoples' words to their thoughts, a troubling concern since Watson (1913, 1920). Spoken language is the data used in protocol analysis, and the richness and variability of language are the greatest assets and liabilities of the verbal reporting methodology. We consider the constructive nature of language comprehension to be one of the greatest ongoing challenges to protocol analysis. When a subject provides verbal reports, there is the built-in language variation that is part of the individual's personality and way of interacting with the world. When a researcher attempts to analyze the verbal report, a separate worldview, vocabulary, and set of inferencing processes is put into action. Despite these constraints, a great deal has been achieved through protocol analysis.

Watson (1920) was concerned with how task parameters might affect verbal reporting. For example, protocol analysis has been used to examine how subjects solve the "Missionaries and Cannibals" problem. A problem-solving subject sitting in a laboratory, describing how missionaries are being ferried from one shore to another to avoid becoming the cannibals' next meal, is working in a problem space with only a few possible actions or moves. Compare this with readers who are asked to report how they construct meaning from a text such as Martin Luther King, Jr.'s "Letter from a Birmingham Jail," or an editorial on raising cigarette taxes. In contrast to the missionaries' options, the range of possible actions during reading is very great. Is it reasonable to assume that self-reports can be as adequate in this more complex situation than in the simple problem-solving situation?

Many continuing concerns with protocol analysis have centered on the related questions of what is requested of subjects, and when it is requested. Watson (1913) directly addressed the first question when he raised concerns about introspection. Introspection occurs when subjects speculate about their actions, their reasons for carrying them out, and narratives of how they carry them out. As a result, subjects report not only the contents of short-term memory, but samples of their theories of mind. Introspective reports can be fascinating and can provide compelling accounts of subjects' thoughts and reflections. Yet, they are generally considered too reflective and too prone to digression to provide firm ground for building theories of on-line cognitive processing, or response to reading. In general, protocol analysis for the purpose of building theory about cognition and response is best served by regular, on-line reports of the contents of short-term memory.

The second concern, when subjects report, has become increasingly informed by our understanding of human information processing and short- and long-term memory. As we explain later, the contents of short-term memory are the fertile ground for verbal reports (Ericsson & Simon, 1984/1993). Because of the limited capacity of short-term memory, and the movement of information and process through it, the recency of verbal reports of cognition and response to their actual occurrence is critical. Like a chance encounter with a stranger's face flashing by in a train window and one's memory of the face, the greater the temporal distance between the event and report, the greater the chance for embellishment or decay of the information. Although this may not mean a less interesting report, it will probably mean a less accurate one.

RELATIONSHIP OF PROTOCOL ANALYSIS TO REIGNING PARADIGMS

Throughout history, protocol analysis has had varied relationships with the reigning psychological paradigms, constructs, and models it was used to investigate. For example, James (1890) regularly relied on introspective reports to inform theories of mind, although perhaps Duncker (1926, 1945) conducted the most famous of the early think-aloud analyses.

Duncker asked people to think aloud as they solved problems. One of the most analyzed of these was the "radiation" problem: A human has an inoperable tumor that can be destroyed by radiation. A ray of sufficient intensity to destroy the tumor, however, would also destroy healthy tissue. How could the tumor be destroyed and yet the healthy tissue preserved? Many of Duncker's subjects provided model think-alouds, in that they reported the contents of short-term memory, revealing their hypotheses and false starts toward a solution, as well as their good progress and eventual solutions. For example, here are the final two self-reports of a subject, after many other possibilities entered consciousness and were dismissed:

> I see no more than two possibilities: either to protect the body or to make the rays harmless. . . .

> Somehow divert . . . diffuse rays . . . disperse . . . stop! Send a broad and a weak bundle of rays through a lens in such a way that the tumor lies at the local (*sic,* focal?) point and thus receives intensive radiation. (Duncker, 1945, p. 3)

This work with protocol analysis, however, seemed to be in need of a theory. Although the data generated in the late 19th and early 20th centuries was important in original form and analysis, there was no formal model of thought processes (e.g., where they come from, what they consist of, how they are generated) that permitted certain interpretation of such data.

The middle part of the 20th century witnessed a relative lull in the use of protocol analysis, as introspection was challenged by behaviorists, beginning with Watson and his contemporaries, whose theories dominated psychology. Behaviorist theory had little need of cognition, for its focus was more on "overt performance than mediating processes" (Ericsson & Simon, 1984/1993). The use of protocol analysis waned for it was fruitless to ask people to report on something that was not considered theoretically important . . . nor did it make sense to use a method that seemed so certain to produce data that could not be believed, data that were merely introspective.

In contrast to behaviorism, the tenets of cognitive psychology and reader response, which began to rise in prominence in the 1960s, can be considered a standing invitation to use protocol analysis. When readers are mindful information processors, who at least sometimes consciously mediate their understanding, it makes sense to expect self-reports that are veridical with ongoing cognitive processes and strategies, to expect that people can report their cognitive and affective responses to text.

From this view, there may be at least three advantages to using protocol analysis: first, it can provide data on cognitive processes and reader responses that otherwise could be investigated only indirectly; second, verbal reports some-times can provide access to the reasoning processes underlying sophisticated cognition, response, and decision making; third, verbal reports allow for the analysis of affective processes of reading in addition to (or in relation to) cognitive processes (Afflerbach & Johnston, 1984). All three types of information are present in the verbal self-reports summarized in this volume.

ERICSSON AND SIMON'S (1984/1993) "PROTOCOL ANALYSIS"

One of the most important events in the development and refinement of protocol analysis was the publication of Ericsson and Simon's *Protocol Analysis: Verbal Reports as Data* in 1984 (revised in 1993). The book summarizes much of the work in protocol analysis and many of the challenges to the methodology, sampling across the domain of cognitive psychology from studies that employ protocol analysis. Ericsson and Simon interpreted protocol analyses with respect to information processing theory, describing conditions when think-aloud data might be expected to be believable and when think-aloud data should be suspect. The volume also includes a definitive review of the evidence (produced up until 1983) that validates the claims about thinking aloud on the basis of information processing theory. After its publication, Ericsson and Simon (1984/1993) became the standard reference on think-aloud methodology.

THEORETICAL UNDERPINNINGS OF THINKING ALOUD

Ericsson and Simon (1984/1993) identified strongly with information processing theory and focused on two constructs in that theory of special importance: long-term memory and short-term memory. Long-term memory contains knowledge of how to do things (i.e., procedural knowledge) as well as a great deal of factual knowledge (i.e., declarative knowledge). Some of the declarative knowledge is episodic knowledge, in that it is memory of some specific event in the thinker's life (e.g., recollection of attending a particular concert). Other knowledge is more generalized, not tied to specific events, but rather representative of types of events in general (e.g., knowledge of what goes on at concerts and in what order). The most important characteristic of long-term memory is that it is vast. Fortunately, it also is organized so that information contained in it can be accessed. Of course, people differ in the degree of organization of the long-term store. For any individual, some types of information will be more organized than other types of information. Thus, a career dentist has extensive and well-organized knowledge of teeth but, typically, less extensive knowledge of automobile engines. The organization of a dentist's knowledge of engines would not approach the sophistication of a mechanic's organization of knowledge of engines. Consequently, when asked about cracks in fillings, the dentist can quickly relate vast knowledge of how such cracks develop, their consequences, and how and when they should be treated. If asked about cracks in engine blocks, the dentist's knowledge is accessed more slowly and is much less complete. Exactly the opposite pattern occurs for mechanics, who can provide detailed commentary about the mechanical relationships in engines that can result in a cracked engine block, but whose memory of cracked fillings is limited to when he or she had one, resulting in the need for a root canal. Ordinarily, a mechanic would not think of a long-past root canal, but that episode can be activated and represented in short-term memory if the environment cues the event (e.g., someone asks the mechanic if he has had a root canal).

The second construct that figures largely in Ericsson and Simon's (1984/1993) work is short-term memory, which is often thought of as information currently in consciousness. The information in short-term memory derives from two sources. One source is external stimulation. For example, if you see a person for the first time and close your eyes to imagine the individual in your mind's eye, the contents of short-term memory reflect stimulation from external sensations. If you begin to think of other people who look like this individual, new names and faces will enter short-term memory. These associations come from your long-term memory, which is the second source of information in short-term memory. Recall the mechanic who had the root canal. The question about the root canal is external stimulation that is coded into short-term memory, with the short-term memory processing of the question cuing long-term memories of the root canal experience.

The consensus view is that short-term memory is extremely limited in capacity, with information leaving short-term memory if the thinker does not operate on it. If a person hears the phone number 725-2276, that number will remain active in short-term memory if the individual repeats it, but will be forgotten rapidly if there is no activity to hold the number sequence in mind. With sufficient rehearsal, or other coding activities, the number may be transferred to long-term memory where it is stored as declarative knowledge.

One especially important property of short-term memory is that people can quickly access the contents of short-term memory and report them. If what is being held is a verbal sequence, then the sequence simply can be verbalized (e.g., "7, 2, 5, 2, 2, 7, 6"). If what is being held is nonverbal (e.g., an image of a cherry red Cadillac convertible), a person can typically verbalize a description of the image. In addition, people are often aware of what they recently held in short-term memory, because some of the contents of short-term memory are translated to long-term memory before they exit short-term awareness. Thus, if a person is asked, "What were you thinking about when you dialed the phone number a minute ago?" often people can recollect what they were thinking about a short time ago. Ericsson and Simon (1984/1993) extensively developed the case that people's reports of the current contents of short-term memory are often valid; they also argued that reports of recent memories (i.e., episodic recollections) are often veridical with what was being reflected on in the recent past. As time passes since the original cognition, the validity of recollections decreases, however. Moreover, the quality of recollections depends on retrieval cues. For example, if asked about your thinking as you made a phone call last night, you might be less likely to remember than if you are reminded that the phone call was to your mother.

In contrast to valid reports of the current contents of short-term memory and recollections of recent episodes, Ericsson and Simon (1984/1993) contended, based on substantial data, that some questions do not stimulate certainly accurate verbal reports. In particular, people typically cannot answer "why" questions, questions about their motives for their behaviors. Thus, if asked, "Why did you call your mother last night?" it is likely that the subject will generate an answer in response to the question, even, if when the call was actually made, the individual was not thinking about why he or she called. Here, Ericsson and Simon's concerns are a clear refrain of those raised about introspection by Watson.

The very best verbal reports, from the Ericsson and Simon (1984/1993) perspective, are of exactly what is heeded in short-term memory. The more that the verbal reports vary from what was heeded, the less certainly believable they are. Thus, if a person is holding in mind, "7-2-5-2-2-7-6," it is believable if they self-report, "7," "2," "5," "2," "2," "7," "6." A report, "I'm holding Steve's phone number in mind," is more suspect, because it does not reflect the exact contents of short-term memory. Nonetheless, Ericsson and Simon (1984/1993) made the case that often such labels of processing represent the processing that occurred, and thus they viewed such self-reports as interpretable. A report, "I'm holding Steve's number in mind because I would have tried so hard to get it," is much less desirable from Ericsson and Simon's (1984/1993) perspective, representing interpretations of thinking on the part of the person making the verbal report.

In short, Ericsson and Simon's (1984/1993) most important conclusion is that people can self-report the contents of their short-term memory. The conclusion provides retrospective validation of think-aloud data gathered in the 1920s and 1930s, data that experienced cycles of acceptance and dismissal until it became more grounded when provided the anchor of the short-term memory model developed by Ericsson and Simon. This position was supported mostly by analysis of think-aloud data, generated in the context of problem solving. In particular, they argued that people can report the intermediate and final products of problem-solving processes with great accuracy, much more certainly than they can detail use of the processes per se. Thus, if a person is adding 1,045 and 2,764 in his or her head, a completely believable self-report would be, "9," "0," "8," "3"—"3,809." Less certainly believable would be labeling of the addition process, rather than reporting of the actual information heeded in short-term memory. Such a report might be, "I'm adding the columns from the right to the left, making certain to keep track of the digits being carried. I'm holding the digits of the solution that I have generated already in mind as I work through the problem from right to left." Ericsson and Simon were explicit that such a description or explanation of process is not as convincing as the reports of the products of processing, arguing that the researcher should infer processes from reports of products rather than encourage their subjects to make such inferences about their processes as part of self-reports. Still, they accepted retrospective descriptions of processes as valid self-reports. Much less believable than descriptions, however, would be the report, "I'm adding column by column because that is how I learned to do it in grade school," which is more an interpretation of one's motivation for processing than a report of the contents of short-term memory. Ericsson and Simon (1984/1993) clearly believed that interpretive descriptions and explanations of cognitive processing were better left to the researcher, who was armed with subject reports of the contents of short-term memory.

One of the most impressive parts of Ericsson and Simon's (1984/1993) book is the section in which they delineated and described introspective, concurrent, and retrospective think-alouds. The careful description of shared characteristics (e.g., all verbal reports are given by subjects related to performing particular tasks) and the important differences (e.g., concurrent reports are given on-line whereas retrospective reports are not) allowed Ericsson and Simon to respond to contemporary critics of verbal self-reports (chapter 1).

Perhaps the tour de force in the Ericsson and Simon (1984/1993) argument is that their perspective is consistent with the positions of even apparent antagonists of verbal reports. For example, Nisbett and Wilson (1977) offered a famous critique of think-aloud data. Ericsson and Simon (1984/1993) managed to establish, however, that even Nisbett and Wilson (1977) concurred with the conclusion that people are able to report the contents of currently activated short-term memory, with the Nisbett and Wilson (1977) critique directed at exactly the types of self-reports that Ericsson and Simon concluded were not available to consciousness and reportable. Ericsson and Simon also made the case that concurrent verbal self-reporting of thinking processes was considered acceptable by John Watson, the same individual who offered the most famous critique of introspective approaches in psychology (see p. 58 of the 1993 edition of Ericsson and Simon's book): "The present writer has often felt that a good deal more can be learned about the psychology of thinking by making subjects think aloud about definite problems, than by trusting to the unscientific method of introspection" (Watson, 1920, p. 91).

SPECIFIC METHODOLOGICAL RECOMMENDATIONS IN ERICSSON AND SIMON (1984/1993)

Through review of the literature on cognitive problem-solving in fairly well-defined domains with clear parameters, Ericsson and Simon (1984/1993) came to a number of conclusions about how self-reports should be collected. These conclusions are important because *in toto*, they have been the state-of-the-science thinking about how to do protocol analyses since the appearance of *Protocol Analysis*. They are also important in this context, because the verbal self-report studies of text processing have varied with respect to how well they have adhered to the various recommendations. Understanding Ericsson and Simon's viewpoint with respect to methodology definitely provides a perspective on what defines a more or less adequate verbal report of a reader's cognitive processing and response.

✓ Think-Aloud Data Should Reflect Exactly What Is Being Thought About. Sometimes, one's thoughts are not fully coherent. The directions given to subjects should make clear that participants should not attempt to make the self-reports more coherent. Although verbalizations of thought processes are not always complete, if the self-report is concurrent, it is, at least, a subset of the information actually heeded in short-term memory when doing the task. It is the researcher's task to make the inferences (and make clear the nature and process of the inferencing), rather than the reader's task to categorize his or her cognitions. Self-reports of nonverbal cognitions (e.g., images) are more likely to be incomplete than self-reports of verbal cognitions, for complex nonverbal cognitions can require many words to describe. Nonverbal cognitions are also generated much more quickly than verbalizations. Still, Ericsson and Simon (1984/1993) argued that verbal self-reports of nonverbal cognitions would reflect many of the properties of the nonverbal cognition.

✓ As People Learn New Procedures and Become Facile with the Procedures, Their Processing Becomes Progressively Automatized. Fully automatic processes are difficult to self-report. They occur very quickly, so much so that intermediate products of processing are not heeded in short-term memory and thus, not available for self-report. Protocol analysis is much more sensitive to processes that have not been automatized, ones that are still under conscious control. One characteristic of controlled processes compared to automatic processes is that they tend to occur sequentially, one step at a time. Thus, their structure is well matched to the structure of verbalizations, which can only report processes in sequence, one at a time.

Ericsson and Simon (1984/1993) had some suggestions for ways of increasing the likelihood of obtaining telling self-reports of otherwise automatized cognition. A researcher might devise procedures to slow the processing down. Thus, for reading, text might be presented sentence by sentence. Another suggestion is to take retrospective reports, perhaps having subjects specify what they were just thinking about in reaction to some type of signal that interrupts processing (e.g., a tone signalling to stop and report the content of one's thoughts or what was just thought about). Ericsson and Simon (1984/1993) particularly recommended these approaches for gaining insights about skilled reading (p. 254) noting they had been used in successful studies of reading that they knew about (e.g., Olson, Mack, & Duffy, 1981; Waern, 1988).

✓ Some Types of Information Are More Likely to Be Represented in Protocols Than Other Types. Whether an idea appears in a think-aloud depends in part on how long it is heeded in short-term memory. For example,

Ericsson and Simon (1984/1993) argued that information about the goal of processing should be more likely to be in self-reports than thoughts that occur rapidly as part of thinking. For example, the goal of finding the distance between two cities given the information in a problem should be more likely to appear in self-reports than fleeting reports of particular numbers used in the intermediate calculations to figure out the distance (p. 257).

Asking Subjects to Provide a Generalized Description of Their Processing Across Trials Is Particularly Problematic. What if their processing changed over trials? The "generalized" description might correspond to efforts on early trials, later trials, or in between. If processing via self-report can only be obtained after a number of items have been processed (e.g., tasks completed), then information is likely to be more valid by cuing the participant with a particular item and requesting report of the processing in connection with that item. Still, the more items and the longer the time that has passed since the probed item was processed, the less well the self-report represents the processing of it that occurred when it was presented originally. One reason that a generalized description may fail to reflect processing across the cycle is that as repetition of a process occurs, some degree of automaticity would be expected to develop. Thus, it may be that only the operations of the early trials were conscious and hence, reportable. A report of whatever processing the subject was conscious of might obscure that the processing was very automatic for many of the trials of the study.

The Directions Given to Think-Aloud Subjects and the Testing Situation Should Be Such as to Discourage Participants from Providing Descriptions or Explanations of Their Processing. The directions should specify clearly that descriptions of explanations of processing are not desired by the researcher and that reports of intermediate and final products of processing are preferred. This leads the subject away from the role of interpreter.

One Reason That Subjects Should Be Discouraged from Self-Reporting Why They Are Carrying Out a Process Is That Such Explanations Have Been Demonstrated to Affect Subsequent Processing. Thus, if people explain why they are solving a problem a certain way, this can affect how they attempt similar problems in the future. When people simply report what they are heeding in short-term memory, it has the potential for increasing memory of that content, but seems less likely to change subsequent processing. Although thinking aloud can slow processing, simply relating the contents of short-term memory does not seem qualitatively to affect processing in other ways. Ericsson and Simon (1984/1993) strongly sent the message that researchers need to think hard about the effects of their think-aloud instruction on processing, for a frequent criticism of the think-aloud methodology is that it changes processing. Fortunately, some forms of think-aloud instructions seem not to change processing much.

Other forms of thinking aloud do shift processing, however. For example, reporting why a process is being used can affect concurrent processing: The sheer amount of cognitive resources needed to explain why a process is being used may crowd short-term memory to the point where all processing is influenced. It can also affect subsequent processing, for example, if the explanation heightens awareness of the effects of the processing.

Directions to Think-Aloud Can Be Rather Open Ended, or They Can Direct Participants to Report a Specific Type of Information That They Have in Working Memory. The nature of the verbal direction given to a subject depends in part on the interests of the researcher. For example, if the researcher is interested in the nature of mental images, the self-report instruction might specify that the participant confine his or her report to images that occur while performing the task in question. Of course, Ericsson and Simon (1984/1993) recognized the potential of such directions to bias processing (e.g., so that many mental images are produced). If the goal is to have as naturalistic cognition as possible, then participants should not be provided information about the particular processes of interest to the researcher. Note, however, that leaving directions open ended means that subjects might feel compelled to report any and all information that they can access in short-term memory. Although this can contribute to rich theory building, it may not address aspects of cognitive processing that are of primary interest to the investigator.

That participants are responsive to researcher directions is a real advantage from the Ericsson and Simon (1984/1993) perspective, one they urged researchers to exploit in crafting directions. Thus, think-aloud directions should emphasize that accuracy of self-reporting is important. They also emphasized that subjects receive feedback if they appear not to be providing careful and complete self-reports. Ericsson and Simon (1984/1993) went so far as urging that researchers make an agreement with their participants to do all possible to be accurate and complete (i.e., honest) in their self-reports. That is, Ericsson and Simon (1984/1993) believed that directions for complete reporting of the contents of short-term memory—directions not to censor self-reports—could go far in over-coming one of the most frequent criticisms of verbal self-reports, that they are incomplete. Such complete reporting might also yield verbal reports that include many thoughts, strategies, and reflections, information richly informative about how cognition and response take place.

In General, People Do Not Require Training in Order to Think Aloud. After examining a number of studies, Ericsson and Simon (1984/1993) concluded that thinking aloud is a natural enough process that lengthy training is not required for adults to be able to carry it out. They did note, however, that as a task proceeds, people sometimes forget to think aloud. Thus, Ericsson and Simon endorsed the use of reminders to subjects to continue to think aloud if a period of time passed without a self-report.

The Last Claim Conflicts a Bit with Another One Made by Ericsson and Simon (1984/1993), That There Are Individual Differences in Ability to Provide Think-Aloud Reports. Unfortunately, Ericsson and Simon provided little analysis or guidance about who should be better able to self-report and who should be disadvantaged, except to note that the ability to self-report probably follows verbal ability in general (see Ericsson & Simon, 1993, p. 250). Different readers may manage their cognitive resources differently, and this can directly impact what is reported and how it is reported.

There Are Also Individual Differences in Thinking. Ericsson and Simon (1993, p. 274) urged researchers not to average over differences in thinking processes, that protocol analysis should reflect the variability between humans in thinking. Summarizing a text or responding to a character in a story are intensely individual processes, and conducting group analyses of such reader–text interactions may wash over important distinctions in individuals' approaches to a task and means of completing the task.

An Important Concern with Any Dependent Variable Is That It Be Reliably Codable. Ericsson and Simon (1984/1993) reported a number of instances of investigators being able to code verbal self-reports into categories reliably. In 1984, which was when they generated their only commentary on this point, there were few examples of researchers inducing categories once data were in hand. Since then, however, there have been studies inspired by grounded theory techniques (e.g., Strauss & Corbin, 1990) in which coding categories have been induced from the data on hand, including some in text processing, so that there are now demonstrations of reliable coding with both a priori categories and induced categories. Ericsson and Simon (1984/1993, chap. 6) made a number of recommendations about how to increase the reliability of protocol data, with most of their recommendations consistent with general principles of measurement.

An Important Part of Demonstrating That a Researcher Understands the Processing That Occurs in a Particular Task Situation Is for the Researcher to Be Able to Predict What People Will Self-Report as They Attempt a Task. Thus, an important part of validating a process model is to make predictions about what processes will be self-verbalized when an individual attempts to do the task in question. A potential challenge in doing this is that processing may vary depending on particular characteristics of the thinker; for example, the prior knowledge of the participant (i.e., there are individual differences in thinking processes as a function of differences in background knowledge). A person knowledgeable about statistics might read a statistics text using different processes than someone who does not have background in statistics. Thus, in order to make accurate predictions about processing that would occur in doing a particular task, it is necessary to understand the task, the state of knowledge of the individual who will be performing the task, and how processing in the task varies with differences in prior knowledge.

In closing this section, we emphasize that by 1993, Ericsson and Simon's thinking on some procedural matters had changed from their perspective in 1984. Particularly important, Ericsson and Simon (1984/1993) reflected awareness that there is great diversity in the directions used to elicit think-alouds, including frequent use of directions inconsistent with their own recommendations. For example, there were many studies in which reports of descriptions of processes were encouraged, and even reports in which explanations of processing were solicited. In reviewing the various studies, Ericsson and Simon (1984/1993) came to the conclusion that such variations in instruction probably did not lead to reliable differences in conclusions across studies. They still contended, however, that when subjects explained their processing or justified it, there was high potential for stimulating shifts in processing. They were quite explicit that self-reports collected with such directions often would not reflect well processing that would occur naturally in the absence of such think-aloud instructions.

In their 1984 volume, Ericsson and Simon devoted much attention to evidence validating think-aloud data (i.e., the self-reports correlated with other indicators of process, such as latency measures). However, by 1993, Ericsson and Simon appeared to believe that the need for such validation was past, with enough validating data in hand to be comfortable with the assumption that verbal self-reports reflected actual processing. We are not so certain—a theme that is taken up in the concluding chapter to this volume.

ERICSSON AND SIMON'S (1984/1993) ENVISIONMENT OF TEXT PROCESSING

When Ericsson and Simon wrote their 1984 book, there was very little work involving think-aloud analyses of reading, especially in contrast to the numerous studies that had been conducted to investigate problem solving. Thus, it is not surprising that the 1984 book contained so little about text processing. Although by 1993 there was much more, Ericsson and Simon (1984/1993) was a minimum revision, involving mostly the addition of a preface, which served to update the book.

What did Ericsson and Simon (1984/1993) conclude about text processing? They argued that with easy text, an instruction to think aloud was tantamount to an instruction to read loud, with very little difference in verbalization between think-aloud and read-aloud instructions (Ericsson & Simon, p. xxxvi; see also Ericsson, 1988). The processes that are easy reading are fully automatized and thus, not available to consciousness for self-report. More difficult texts result in slower reading, consciously controlled reading. The result is "substantial verbalization of information not explicitly given in the text" (p. xxxvi). Consistent with

Kintsch (1988), Ericsson and Simon's (1993) view was that conscious processing besides decoding is not necessary in order for readers to understand easy texts. Active and strategic efforts at meaning construction only occur in reaction to more challenging texts.

They were particularly struck that Trabasso and Suh (1993) were able to demonstrate predictive relationships between the processes subjects reported during thinking-aloud and detailed understanding of text (e.g., reports of elaboration were correlated with behavioral measures reflecting inferential processing). In general, the Trabasso and Suh (1993) outcomes were consistent with Ericsson and Simon's (1984/1993) expectation that meaning construction above the word level was more likely to occur via conscious efforts, ones that could be reflected in verbal self-reports, than was skilled decoding:

> Our earlier discussion of text comprehension by adults showed that recognition of individual words is direct, while the integration of the information in a given sentence of a text requires successful retrieval of relevant information presented earlier in the text along with prior knowledge and bridging inferences accessed from the subject's long-term memory. The process of integration is mediated and thus, reportable. (Ericsson & Simon, 1984/1993, p. xiii)

What may be especially surprising to readers of a volume dedicated to think-aloud reports during text processing is that Ericsson and Simon (1984/1993) were pessimistic about obtaining reasonably complete reports of cognitive activities during reading: "Subjects reading text or attempting to understand written problem descriptions sometimes give rather scanty and uninformative thinking-aloud protocols . . ." (1993, p. 252); "when subjects think aloud while reading, little more than the text itself is vocalized . . ." (1993, p. 254). The case made throughout this volume is that Ericsson and Simon's (1984/1993) pessimism on this point was unjustified, with it now possible to specify the conscious processes of reading in detail because of think-aloud reports.

2

▼▼▼▼▼▼▼

Methods Employed to Construct a Summary of Conscious Processes During Skilled Reading

Our general purpose when we began this book was to identify and describe exhaustively the many processes, including strategies and responses, that readers carry out consciously as they read. That is, what decisions can readers make when they read? What can they decide to do in order to come to terms with text? How do readers control the reading of text? Our most important assumption was that such processes are reflected by think-aloud protocols. We believed that the protocol analyses generated since the 1970s would have a depth and breadth to allow us to adequately chart diverse aspects of skilled reading.

The purpose of this chapter is to review the methods that were employed in this analysis and to detail the challenges in summarizing the active life of the reader as reflected in the think-alouds. We present as well a synopsis of how we dealt with those challenges. At the center of this analysis were the studies contributing data to it and thus, an appropriate starting point for this chapter on analysis is a review of the characteristics of the studies summarized here.

THE THINK-ALOUD RESEARCH LITERATURE

The first challenge was to assemble the relevant literature. Because both of us had published think-aloud analyses, we had many of the most relevant studies in our file drawers and thus, that was our starting point. We reviewed these studies, noting especially references to other think-aloud analyses and articles about think-aloud that were not in our files. The missing articles were retrieved.

The group of papers on hand at this point were from diverse literatures, from rhetoric to cognitive psychology to reader response to reading education. Our next move was to survey the journal and volume indices (by hand) of the disciplines represented, covering material since the early 1980s. In addition, we talked with other researchers who had conducted think-aloud studies of skilled reading to solicit information about studies we might have missed. As this project proceeded and we presented preliminary results in different settings (e.g., 1992 and 1993 National Reading Conferences, colloquium presentations), members of our audiences occasionally offered information about studies we had overlooked.

The challenges of dealing with this literature became ever more apparent once a large sample of studies was identified. The main difficulties were as follows, along with our tactics for dealing with them:

1. Not all of the articles identified represented primary research. Protocol analysis is a controversial method of research and thus, a number of papers have been published reviewing the strengths and weaknesses of protocol analyses. We decided to rely principally on the primary research studies for information about the conscious processing and responding that occurs during reading. Still, the review papers were carefully studied at various points in our analyses to determine if they added any information to our overview and thus, these articles are included in the reference list of sources consulted as part of our analyses. Where these review papers informed the summary list of processes covered in the next chapter, they are appropriately cited. Still, we emphasize that the analyses contributing the most to our summary of processes were the primary research studies, reflecting that our attention throughout the writing of this book was much more directed at primary data rather than secondary sources.

2. The reading tasks studied in protocol analyses have varied greatly. Particularly relevant at this point, some of the reading tasks have been much more like natural reading than others, with natural reading involving the processing of intact texts. The more natural the text, the better from our perspective. Although it was easy to decide that tasks involving reading of texts with missing words or letters (e.g., Kletzien, 1991, 1992; Rauenbusch & Bereiter, 1991), purely logical texts (e.g., Deffner, 1988), reading of test items (Norris, 1990, 1992), and search of tables and "paragraphs" comprised of concatenations of factual information were not natural from this perspective (e.g., Guthrie, Britten, & Barker, 1991); others were more borderline, such as when readers in Trabasso and Suh (1993) read a number of texts with very particular logical structures. In general, only a very few texts/tasks were eliminated based on this criterion. Even so, once a solid, first-run draft of readers' conscious processing was available, these eliminated studies were examined to determine if there were any reader behaviors represented in these studies that should be added to the summary. Guthrie et al. (1991), for example, was notable in adding information about how people can search during reading. Thus, the final list of primary-research studies informing

our summary of conscious processing includes Guthrie et al. (1991; see Table 2.1).

3. The 38 primary research studies that most informed our summary of conscious processing were varied in a number of ways. As is summarized in Table 2.1, the types of readers varied. The youngest readers were included in Phillips' (1988) study of sixth-grade readers; the most proficient readers were PhDs, professors, and other professionals (Afflerbach, 1990b; Bazerman, 1985; Bereiter & Bird, 1985; Charney, 1993; Graves & Frederiksen, 1991; Lundeberg, 1987; Wineberg, 1991; Wyatt et al., 1993). Studies of high school, undergraduate, and graduate students provided samples presumably of varied reader proficiency. Still, there was a heavy bias in these studies toward good readers. For example, none of the participants in these studies seemed to have decoding difficulties; many of the studies involved readers with years of experience with the type of text being read. We have little doubt that the totality of processes summarized in this book reflects conscious processing during reading.

The texts varied in how well they matched the reader's expertise. Sometimes, there was a good match of the text with the particular area of reader expertise. Sometimes, texts were selected that were definitely not consistent with the content area expertise of readers. In addition, these studies included a variety of text types, including poems, narratives, and expositions (see Table 2.1).

In short, the readers, texts, and tasks in the primary research studies were diverse. We view this situation as a strength. Our goal was to summarize all available conscious processes. Thus, a reasonable expectation is that the greater the range of readers and texts in the focus studies, the greater the range of processes that would be represented in the processes reported in the studies. Even so, as the discussion of these studies proceeds, especially the ways in which these studies were diverse, it becomes more obvious that the diversity in these investigations made it impossible to construct any easy-to-apply algorithm that would summarize outcomes across studies (e.g., like a quantitative meta-analysis).

4. Because the focus studies were generated by investigators from diverse disciplines, diverse reporting standards were represented in the sample of studies. Thus, the sample includes decidedly qualitative studies, such as those reported by rhetoricians (e.g., Bazerman, 1985; Charney, 1993) and some educational researchers (e.g., Wineberg, 1991), although various types of quantitative analyses were employed in the majority of studies. The challenge with the quantitative studies is that the quantitative analyses were also very diverse, from very conventional (e.g., Earthman, 1989) to extremely unconventional, such as Wyatt et al.'s (1993) quantification of their generally qualitative analysis.

5. The different investigators were interested in different aspects of processing. Often, the starting point was a search for the strategies used by readers. Even so, conceptions of strategies differed tremendously from investigator to investigator. For example, the rhetoricians were more interested in reader evaluation processes than were the cognitive scientists. Some of the investigators

TABLE 2.1
Most Important Primary Studies Used in This Analysis

Study	Participants	Texts Read
Afflerbach (1990a)	Five graduate students familiar with think-aloud process and reading comprehension process literature; five graduate students not familiar with thinking aloud or reading process literature; five 11th-grade students in gifted and talented literature program	Three essays, two short stories (three of five used previously in Olson et al., 1981, study)
Afflerbach (1990b)	Four anthropology and four chemistry doctoral students	One 600-word introductory section from an anthropology journal article; one 600-word introductory section from a chemistry journal article
Bazerman (1985)	Seven physicists	Journal articles of their own selection in their areas of interest/expertise
Beach (1972)	Thirty-six upper class English majors	Three contemporary poems
Bereiter & Bird (1985)	Two psychology graduate students, eight middle-class professionals	Six 500-word passages (an exposition, a description, a narrative, an opinion, a controversy, a process description)
Caron (1989)	Ten university undergraduates, all reading at Grade 14 reading level or better	Excerpts from three expository articles
Charney (1993)	5 ecologists, 1 paleontologist, 1 anthropologist	An article attacking evolutionary biology
Christopherson, Shultz, & Waern (1981)	Thirty-five high school students	Passage (181 words long) that is difficult to understand without title; 10 subjects read with title, 25 read without it
Collins, Brown, & Larkin (1980)	Four college students	Five short, difficult-to-understand passages (read to subjects)
Deegan (1993)	Ten first-year law students who were doing well in law school, 10 first-year law students experiencing difficulties in law school	A single law review article (1,400 words long)

(Continued)

TABLE 2.1
(Continued)

Study	Participants	Texts Read
Earthman (1989, 1992)	Eight undergraduate students, 8 graduate students in English	Two short stories, 2 poems
Fletcher (1986)	Thirty undergraduate psychology students	10 short stories, 10 short news articles
Goldman & Saul (1990)	Thirty-two introductory psychology students, 16 native English speakers, 16 ESL speakers	Sixteen 350–450-word passages from introductory-level college textbooks
Graves & Frederiksen (1991)	Two senior English professors, six college sophomores enrolled in an English literature course	Four-page excerpt from *The Color Purple*
Guthrie, Britten, & Barker (1991)	Twenty-five undergraduate students	A table from an almanac, a directory with information presented in paragraphs (participants asked to find particular pieces of information in these sources)
Haas & Flower (1988)	Four graduate students, 6 college freshmen	Part of the preface of an undergraduate psychology text
Hare (1981)	University undergraduate students, 12 were good readers, 12 were poor readers	One easy article from a domain familiar to the students, one technical article from a domain not familiar to the students
Johnston & Afflerbach (1985)	Two graduate students, one assistant professor	Four short articles outside of fields of expertise
Kintgen (1983)	Six advanced graduate students in English	Three poems
Kucan (1993)	Three 6th-grade boys, A– to B+ students	Expository excerpt (456 words)
Lundeberg (1987)	Eight law professors, two attorneys, 10 at least graduate-level adults in fields besides law	One 1,100-word legal case, one 1,500-word legal case
Lytle (1982)	Twenty-one 6th-grade students varying in verbal ability as defined by verbal SAT	One 158-word passage from the SAT verbal section, one 218-word letter to the editor of *Manchester Guardian*, one 1,500-word chapter from Lewis Thomas' *The Lives of a Cell*

(Continued)

TABLE 2.1
(Continued)

Study	Participants	Texts Read
Meyers, Lytle, Palladino, Devenpeck, & Green (1990)	Twenty-seven 4th-grade students and nine 5th-grade students, all average or better than average readers	Three narrative passages, 16 to 21 sentences long
Olshavsky (1976–1977)	Twelve good 10th-grade readers, 12 poor 10th-grade readers	Four short stories: one interesting/concrete; one interesting/abstract; one not interesting/concrete; one not interesting/abstract
Olson, Mack, & Duffy (1981)	College students	Four short essays, two short stories
Phillips (1988)	Forty low-proficiency, 40 high-proficiency 6th-grade readers	Three short passages on familiar topics, three on unfamiliar topics
Pritchard (1990a)	Proficient 11th-grade readers, 30 from U.S., 30 from Palua	Two short passages, one about American funerals, one about Paluan funerals, so one passage culturally familiar and one culturally unfamiliar for each reader
Rogers (1991)	Eight 9th-grade students	Faulkner story, "A Rose for Emily"
Schmalhofer & Boschert (1988)	Twenty-two undergraduate psychology students	Study 1: Six-paragraph text about LISP programming language and/or 42 LISP examples accompanied by 10 sentences; Study 2: Subset of Study 1 materials
Schwegler & Shamoon (1991)	Eight sociologists	Slightly altered sociology student papers
Shearer, Coballes-Vega, & Lundeberg (1993)	Twelve professionally active teachers with master's degree	One professional article, selected by reader as something they planned to read
Squire (1964)	Fourteen- to 16-year-olds, 27 males, 15 females	Four short stories
Trabasso & Suh (1993)	Eight undergraduate students	Eight pairs of stories, with each story having a definite causal structure

(Continued)

TABLE 2.1
(Continued)

Study	Participants	Texts Read
Wade, Trathen, & Schraw (1990)	Sixty-seven undergraduate students	Chapter from Carson's *The Sea Around Us*
Wineberg (1991)	Eight historians, eight high-ability high school students	Excerpts from original historical documents and history texts
Wood & Zakaluk (1992)	Twelve teachers (six elementary, six secondary)	Two demanding passages from professional journals, one in literary criticism, one in plant biology
Wyatt et al. (1993)	Fifteen social sciences professors	Professional-level articles in their area of interest/expertise

came to their protocol analyses intent to look for particular strategies, processes, and responses, whereas others were intent to construct their categories of processing from the ground up, reporting, as much as possible, whatever processing readers elected to use. A positive spin can be put on this situation from our perspective: If a single model of processing and reader interaction with text, or even if very few models had driven most of the studies, the conscious processing detected would have been heavily biased toward the processes represented in the models tested. A reasonable expectation is that more processes would be detected across studies when many models of processing were tested across studies. One of the reasons that so many processes are reported in the next chapter is that investigators have looked for a wide variety of processes.

6. The specific operations involved in collecting think-aloud data varied tremendously from study to study. About the only common operation across these studies was that participant verbalizations were tape recorded, although even that claim is tentative because some of the methods descriptions were very incomplete! Here are some of the ways that operations in the studies differed:

a. Although authorities such as Ericsson and Simon (1984/1993) specified that think-alouds should be reports of the content of thought (i.e., a statement of exactly what is being thought) rather than reader interpretation of processes or responses (e.g., a claim that, "I'm summarizing here," or, "I'm interpreting when I say this is about . . ."), very few of the studies adhered to such a criterion. In fact, it was common in these studies for the researchers to direct their subjects to report their "processes," "strategies," and "why they are doing what they are doing." Most critical here, however, is that the studies varied greatly in what readers were asked to report aloud.

b. The studies also varied with respect to reader goals. Sometimes readers were instructed to read as they would in preparation for a test. Sometimes they were to read naturally (to the degree that this is possible under think-aloud protocol analysis conditions). Sometimes they were to read so they could use the information they derived from text however they would normally use it.

c. The studies varied with respect to familiarity with think-aloud processes and practice in thinking aloud. For example, five of the readers in Afflerbach (1990a) were professionally knowledgable about thinking aloud and skilled reading comprehension processes. In contrast, most participants in other investigations had no prestudy familiarity with thinking aloud. In Afflerbach's studies, participants were briefed about thinking aloud a week before their participation in the studies so that they could reflect on their reading processes in anticipation of generating think-alouds. This period of anticipation was followed by explicit practice in thinking aloud immediately before the critical data were collected, which was typical in the focus studies. Although typical, it was not universal, however, with some investigators not providing any practice. When practice occurred, it was usually brief, involving one or a few passages, with practice reported in terms of minutes. Although practice typically involved thinking aloud while reading, in some studies subjects practiced thinking aloud with other tasks, typically performing mathematics problems (i.e., the researchers borrowed practice tasks from the traditional protocol analysis literature represented in Ericsson & Simon, 1984/1993).

d. The studies varied tremendously in the care taken to avoid biasing participants with respect to reported processes. At the one extreme, as part of instructions, the researcher modeled thinking aloud, providing some information about what the reader might do. Afflerbach (1990a) told participants that he was interested in their predictions, elaborations, and inferences. Graves and Frederiksen (1991) told their subjects they wanted them to comment on the content and style of the text read. Haas and Flower (1988) instructed their readers to interpret the text. Schwegler and Shamoon (1991) called on their readers to evaluate what they were reading and to report their evaluations. At the other extreme, the researchers made absolutely no comment on what processes might be reported. Somewhere in the middle was a study like Lundeberg (1987), in which the readers were asked to be like a teacher in their report of processing, revealing their thought processes as a teacher would to a student. Why the variability in directions? In general, it was because the investigators were interested in different processes and different aspects of reading, and probably believed that a particular request or series of requests would get them what they were looking for.

e. Although Ericsson and Simon (1984/1993) emphasized that verbalizations are most valid if they are concurrent, the studies varied widely about when processes were reported. In some studies they were concurrent. In others, they were required after each sentence, after each episode, at signaled spots in text, at least every 2 minutes, at the end of the reading, or whenever readers wanted to make them. The result is that reports were given with various degrees of concurrency.

Although one justifiable reaction to these many variations in methods might be exasperation and an accompanying declaration that no definitively valid claims could emanate from such a diverse pack of investigations, we were not exasperated. Rather, our view was that the variability across studies should have increased the variability in processes reported and hence, increased the likelihood that all of conscious processes that are possible during reading would have occurred in one or more studies.

(In summary), our search of the literature turned up 38 primary studies that contributed substantially to the analysis reported here, all of which are cited in Table 2.1. Some review papers and conceptual overviews were identified as well, as were some studies involving thinking aloud, but with respect to tasks other than natural reading. The secondary analyses and primary analyses of phenomena related to reading did not contribute to the analysis reported here as greatly as the articles listed in Table 2.1, but these sources were reviewed to determine if any processes were cited in them that should be added to our summary. (All analyses of thinking-aloud during reading that were examined in preparation of this volume are included in the bibliography that concludes this chapter.) No additional processes were identified through this examination of secondary articles, although having the processes included in our summary featured in the secondary analyses bolstered our confidence in the summary reported in the next chapter. We emphasize, however, that the summary reported in the next chapter is much more complete than any previously reported overview of conscious processes during reading. What we take up next is how we came to that summary from the starting point of the studies summarized in Table 2.1.

THE ANALYSIS OF THE PRIMARY RESEARCH STUDIES

The analysis reported here was of the many processes reported in the think-aloud studies listed in Table 2.1. That is, the reported processes were the data, with each process in a study a data point. Pressley's intent was to do a grounded analysis of the data, following as closely as possible the prescriptions of Strauss and Corbin (1990). The intention was to sift the data from the ground up in order to come to a theory of the data—in order to identify meaningful dimensions in the data and how the dimensions relate to one another. Ideally, the researcher moves from case to case until no new insights are being generated. This ideal was met to some extent.

Pressley conducted the analysis in the first instance, with Afflerbach cross-checking and auditing Pressley's analysis at various points in the process. Because we had both conducted think-aloud analyses, ones included in Table 2.1, we were anything but blank slates as we began the task. That is, we both held preconceived notions of the dimensions of reading processes. Although nothing could be done to erase such memories and conceptions, we attempt to portray as fairly as possible our prior knowledge-based biases.

Afflerbach came to the effort with experiences from a series of think-aloud studies (Afflerbach, 1990a; Afflerbach, 1990b; Johnston & Afflerbach, 1985) that was preceded by a critical review of the think-aloud method in reading research (Afflerbach & Johnston, 1984). These investigations focused on the strategies of accomplished readers as they constructed main ideas, and as they worked through main idea tasks with varied levels of prior knowledge for the text topic. More recently, Afflerbach used think-alouds to study teachers' problem solving related to classroom assessments (Afflerbach & Johnston, 1993). Thus, Afflerbach had varied experiences with verbal reports used in the investigation of reading strategies, text interpretation, literacy assessment, and problem-solving.

Pressley used protocol analyses in his research on memory (e.g., Pressley & Levin, 1977; Pressley, Levin, & Ghatala, 1988). He came to the task of preparing this volume having recently completed the Wyatt et al. (1993) study. The major finding in that investigation was that social sciences professors reading professional-level articles in their areas of expertise and interest engaged in strategic processes, monitoring, and evaluation. This finding was contrasted with the conclusions of think-aloud studies reported by cognitive scientists, who tended to report strategies and monitoring but not evaluations, and rhetoricians, who tended to report reader evaluations. An important hypothesis to emerge from the study, based on a very strong correlation between reader monitoring activities and their evaluations, was that monitoring and evaluation are closely tied (e.g., perhaps the awareness that is monitoring permits evaluations).

Given the recent experience with Wyatt et al. (1993), which had been conceived, analyzed, interpreted, and written in light of much of the literature summarized in Table 2.1, Pressley expected that he might find strategies, monitoring, and evaluations in the think-aloud analyses when he went through the Table 2.1 data base systematically. That, in fact, occurred, but only after much reflection on the entire body of processes reported in the studies in Table 2.1.

To begin the analysis, Pressley read all of the studies in his hands in November, 1992. That is, some of the studies summarized in Table 2.1 had not been found yet. Every process reported in every investigation was recorded, one process report to an index card. These cards were arranged in several different ways. For one, Pressley attempted to identify synonymous processes and replace several cards reporting the same process with one card. Once a great deal of redundancy was eliminated, Pressley looked for sensible ways to organize the various processes. What was most salient was that the three-part division identified when much of this same literature had been reviewed as part of the Wyatt et al. (1993) project was apparent when all of the studies were inventoried systematically. There were reports of strategies, monitoring, and evaluation in these studies, and thus, an initial classification was put together based on this three-part division.

It was apparent that the processes within each of these three broad classifications could be divided further and thus, once three large piles were created,

Pressley turned attention to identification of clusters. By the middle of 1992, a preliminary analysis was prepared. At that point, Afflerbach reviewed the analysis for internal consistency and possible redundancy and felt enough progress had been made to unveil the preliminary analysis at the 1992 National Reading Conference. It was also determined that a fourth category of report was emerging from the wealth of think-aloud data: the social aspects and contexts of reading.

In the months that followed, Pressley reviewed the classifications many times additionally, shuffling categories to improve the fit, adding some new processes as new studies were identified, read, and added to the analysis. By late summer 1993, Afflerbach once again reviewed the resulting structure for internal consistency and redundancy, again approving of the summary at that point. Still additional shuffling took place with additional reflection in the fall of 1993, a period when the last studies identified were added to the analysis. In early 1994, Pressley turned the entire analysis over to Afflerbach for a careful audit, including an attempt to verify that each process specified was actually reported in one or more of the think-aloud analyses of reading in the literature. Later in spring 1994, we both conferred to consider those parts of the summary that one or the other still considered to be problematic. The "most gray" area involved the social nature of reading, and the fact that although few researchers asked their readers to report on the social aspects of their reading, the reports filtered through nevertheless. A decision was made to acknowledge and examine the social context of reading that influenced readers' verbal reports. It was also decided that because few studies sought verbal reports on the social aspects of reading, the spontaneous nature of most socially oriented verbal reports must be considered from two perspectives. First, because of their spontaneity such reports are assumed to be veridical: they provide flashes of the social world that the reader operates in. Second, because of their random occurrence, such reports are probably not an adequate foundation on which to build more than an educated guess of theory.

At the end of this process, we agreed that the summary reported in the next chapter is as complete and coherent as we could make it—for now. The "for now" is an important reservation and brings the discussion back to the ideal of grounded theory analysis that was partially met here. A grounded analysis should continue until the theory is *saturated*, to use Strauss and Corbin's (1990) term meaning that new data do not result in changes to the theory. We were partially successful in reaching saturation in that by the end of the enterprise new studies that were identified did not result in profound changes in the summary, but rather very minor adjustments. Still, that there were minor adjustments made clear that the theory was not fully saturated. Thus, we expect that with additional reflection in the future, especially as new primary studies become available, there will be need to modify the summary reported in the next chapter. More positively, although we recognize that others might come up with other ways of organizing the processes summarized in the next chapter, we believe it unlikely based on the available data that anyone would succeed in identifying important processes that were overlooked in our reading of the articles and construction of a summary. That is, we expect to modify our summary accretionally in future years.

Even so, we recognize that some other individual or team might succeed in constructing a grounded theory using the same data that would be very different from the theory summarized in the next chapter. In fact, we hope that others will try to do so with the corpus of processes included in the next chapter, believing it might be extremely heuristic for text processing research if there were two or several competing grounded theories of the processes comprising skilled reading. Such a situation would almost certainly be a stimulus for additional inquiry, which would expand the knowledge base even more and permit ever more refined and complete theories in the future. For the present, however, we proceed to the not-quite-saturated theory that emerged from our analysis efforts based on the data in hand in early 1994.

BIBLIOGRAPHY OF STUDIES/SECONDARY ANALYSES USED TO CONSTRUCT THE SUMMARY OF READING COMPREHENSION PROCESSES[1]

*Afflerbach, P. (1990a). The influence of prior knowledge and text genre on readers' prediction strategies. *Journal of Reading Behavior, 22,* 131–148.

*Afflerbach, P. (1990b). The influence of prior knowledge on expert readers' main idea construction strategies. *Reading Research Quarterly, 25,* 31–46.

Afflerbach, P., & Johnston, P. (1984). Research methodology: On the use of verbal reports in reading research. *Journal of Reading Behavior, 16,* 307–322.

*Bazerman, C. (1985). Physicists reading physics: Schema-laden purposes and purpose-laden schema. *Written Communication, 2,* 3–24.

*Beach, R. W. (1972). *The literary response process of college students while reading and discussing three poems.* Doctoral dissertation, University of Illinois (*Dissertation Abstracts International* Order No. 73-17112).

*Bereiter, C., & Bird, M. (1985). Use of thinking aloud in identification and teaching of reading comprehension strategies. *Cognition and Instruction, 2,* 131–156.

Bridge, C., & Winograd, P. (1982). Readers' awareness of cohesive relationships during cloze comprehension. *Journal of Reading Behavior, 14,* 299–312.

Brown, A., & Day, J. (1983). Macrorules for summarizing strategies: The development of expertise. *Journal of Verbal Learning and Verbal Behavior, 22,* 1–14.

*Caron, T. A. (1989). Strategies for reading expository prose. In S. McCormick & J. Zutell (Eds.), *Cognitive and social perspectives for literacy research and instruction, 38th yearbook of the National Reading Conference* (pp. 293–300). Chicago: National Reading Conference.

*Charney, D. (1993). A study in rhetorical reading: How evolutionists read "The Spaniards of San Marco." In J. Selzer (Ed.), *Understanding scientific prose.* Madison WI: University of Wisconsin Press.

*Christopherson, S. L., Schultz, C. B., & Waern, Y. (1981). The effect of two contextual conditions on recall of a reading passage and on thought processes in reading. *Journal of Reading, 24,* 573–578.

---

[1]Asterisks indicate primary studies.

*Collins, A. M., Brown, J. S., & Larkin, K. M. (1980). Inferences in text understanding. In R. J. Spiro, B. C. Bruce, & W. F. Brewer (Eds.), *Theoretical issues in reading comprehension* (pp. 385–407). Hillsdale, NJ: Lawrence Erlbaum Associates.

*Deegan, D. H. (1993, December). *Exploring the relations among reading strategies, comprehension, and performance in a specific domain: The case of law.* Paper presented at the annual meeting of the National Reading Conference, Charleston.

Deffner, G. (1988). Concurrent thinking aloud: An on-line tool for studying representations used in text understanding. *Text, 8,* 351–367.

*Earthman, E. A. (1989). *The lonely, quiet concert: Readers creating meaning from literary texts.* Unpublished doctoral dissertation, Stanford University, School of Education, Stanford.

*Earthman, E. A. (1992). Creating the virtual work: Readers' processes in understanding literary texts. *Research in the Teaching of English, 26,* 351–384.

Ericsson, K. A. (1988). Concurrent verbal reports on text comprehension: A review. *Text, 8,* 295–325.

*Fletcher, C. R. (1986). Strategies for the allocation of short-term memory during comprehension. *Journal of Memory and Language, 25,* 43–58.

Garner, R. (1982). Verbal-report data on reading strategies. *Journal of Reading Behavior, 14,* 159–167.

Geisler, C. (1991). Toward a sociocognitive model of literacy: Constructing mental models in philosophical conversation. In C. Bazerman & J. Paradis (Eds.), *Textual dynamics of the professions* (pp. 171–190). Madison: University of Wisconsin Press.

*Goldman, S. R., & Saul, E. U. (1990). Flexibility in text processing: A strategy competition model. *Learning and Individual Differences, 2,* 181–219.

*Graves, B., & Frederiksen , C. H. (1991). Literary expertise in the description of fictional narrative. *Poetics, 20,* 1–26.

*Guthrie, J., Britten, T., & Barker, K. (1991). Roles of document structure, cognitive strategy, and awareness in searching for information. *Reading Research Quarterly, 26,* 300–324.

*Haas, C., & Flower, L. (1988). Rhetorical reading strategies and the construction of meaning. *College Composition and Communication, 39,* 167–183.

*Hare, V. C. (1981). Readers' problem identification and problem solving strategies for high- and low-knowledge articles. *Journal of Reading Behavior, 13,* 359–365.

Hoffstaedter, P. (1987). Poetic text processing and its empirical investigation. *Poetics, 16,* 75–91.

*Johnston, P., & Afflerbach, P. (1985). The process of constructing main ideas from text. *Cognition and Instruction, 2,* 207–232.

Kavale, K., & Schreiner, R. (1979). The reading processes of above average and average readers: A comparison of the use of reasoning strategies in responding to standardized comprehension measures. *Reading Research Quarterly, 15,* 102–128.

*Kintgen, E. R. (1983). *The perception of poetry.* Bloomington: Indiana University Press.

Kletzien, S. B. (1991). Strategy use by good and poor comprehenders reading expository text of differing levels. *Reading Research Quarterly, 26,* 67–86.

Kletzien, S. B. (1992). Proficient and less proficient comprehenders' strategy use for different top-level structures. *Journal of Reading Behavior, 24,* 191–215.

*Kucan, L. (1993, December). *Uncovering cognitive processes in reading.* Paper presented at the annual meeting of the National Reading Conference, Charleston.

*Lundeberg, M. A. (1987). Metacognitive aspects of reading comprehension: Studying understanding in legal case analysis. *Reading Research Quarterly, 22,* 407–432.

*Lytle, S. L. (1982). *Exploring comprehension style: A study of twelfth-grade readers' transactions with texts.* Doctoral dissertation, University of Pennsylvania (University Microfilms No. 82-27292).

Magliano, J. P., & Graesser, A. C. (1993). A three-pronged method for studying inference generation in literary text. *Poetics, 20,* 193–232.

Marr, M. (1983, April). *Verbal reports: How readers process unfamiliar texts.* Paper presented at the annual meeting of the American Educational Research Association, Montreal.

*Meyers, J., Lytle, S., Palladino, D., Devenpeck, G., & Green, M. (1990). Think-aloud protocol analysis: An investigation of reading comprehension strategies in fourth- and fifth-grade students. *Journal of Psychoeducational Assessment, 8*, 112–127.

Mulcahy-Ernt, P. (1991, December). *Reader strategies for comprehending concepts in biology text.* Paper presented at the National Reading Conference, Palm Springs, CA.

Norris, S. P. (1990). Effect of eliciting verbal reports of thinking on critical thinking test performance. *Journal of Educational Measurement, 27*, 41–58.

Norris, S. P. (1992). A demonstration of the use of verbal reports of thinking in multiple-choice critical thinking test design. *Alberta Journal of Educational Research, 38*, 153–176.

Norris, S. P., & Phillips, L. M. (1987). Explanations of reading comprehension: Schema theory and critical thinking theory. *Teachers College Record, 89*, 281–306.

*Olshavsky, J. E. (1976–1977). Reading as problem solving: An investigation of strategies. *Reading Research Quarterly, 12*, 654–674.

Olson, G. M., Duffy, S. A., & Mack, R. L. (1984). Thinking-out-loud as a method for studying real-time comprehension processes. In D. E. Kieras & M. A. Just (Eds.), *New methods in reading comprehension research* (pp. 253–286). Hillsdale, NJ: Lawrence Erlbaum Associates.

*Olson, G. M., Mack, R. L., & Duffy, S. A. (1981). Cognitive aspects of genre. *Poetics, 10*, 283–315.

*Phillips, L. M. (1988). Young readers' inference strategies in reading comprehension. *Cognition and Instruction, 5*, 193–222.

Phillips, L. M., & Norris, S. P (1987). Reading well is thinking well. In N. C. Burbules (Ed.), *Philosophy of education 1986* (pp. 187–197). Normal, IL: Philosophy of Education Society.

*Pritchard, R. (1990a). The effects of cultural schemata on reading processing strategies. *Reading Research Quarterly, 25*, 273–295.

Pritchard, R. (1990b). The evolution of introspective methodology and its implications for studying the reading process. *Reading Psychology: An International Quarterly, 11*, 1–13.

Rauenbusch, F., & Bereiter, C. (1991). Making reading more difficult: A degraded text microworld for teaching reading comprehension strategies. *Cognition and Instruction, 8*, 181–206.

*Rogers, T. (1991). Students as literary critics: The interpretive experiences, beliefs, and processes of ninth-grade students. *Journal of Reading Behavior, 23*, 391–423.

*Schmalhofer, F., & Boschert, S. (1988). Differences in verbalization during knowledge acquisition from texts and discovery learning from example situations. *Text, 8*, 369–393.

*Schwegler, R. A., & Shamoon, L. K. (1991). Meaning attribution in ambiguous texts in sociology. In C. Bazerman & J. Paradis (Eds.), *Textual dynamics of the professions* (pp. 216–233). Madison: University of Wisconsin Press.

*Shearer, B., Coballes-Vega, C., & Lundeberg, M. (1993, December). *How do teachers who are professionally active select, read, and use professional journals?* Paper presented at the annual meeting of the National Reading Conference, Charleston.

Smagorinsky, P. (1989). The reliability and validity of protocol analysis. *Written Communication, 6*, 463–479.

*Squire, J. R. (1964). *The responses of adolescents while reading four short stories.* Champaign, IL: National Council of Teachers of English.

Steen, G. (1991). The empirical study of literary reading: Methods of data collection. *Poetics, 20*, 559–575.

*Trabasso, T., & Suh, S. (1993). Understanding text: Achieving explanatory coherence through on-line inferences and mental operations in working memory. *Discourse Processes, 16*, 3–34.

Wade, S. E. (1990). Using think alouds to assess comprehension. *The Reading Teacher, 43*, 442–451.

*Wade, S. E., Trathen, W., & Schraw, G. (1990). An analysis of spontaneous study strategies. *Reading Research Quarterly, 25*, 147–166.

Waern, Y. (1988). Thoughts on text in context: Applying the think-aloud method to text processing. *Text, 8*, 327–350.

*Wineberg, S. S. (1991). On the reading of historical texts: Notes on the breach between school and academy. *American Educational Research Journal, 28*, 495–520.

*Wood, B., & Zakaluk, B. (1992, December). *The main ideas comprehension processing of teachers as expert readers*. Paper presented at the National Reading Conference, San Antonio.

*Wyatt, D., Pressley, M., El-Dinary, P. B., Stein, S., Evans, P., & Brown, R. (1993). Reading behaviors of domain experts processing professional articles that are important to them: The critical role of worth and credibility monitoring. *Learning and Individual Differences, 5*, 49–72.

3

▼▼▼▼▼▼▼

What Readers Can Do When They Read: A Summary of the Results from the On-Line Self-Report Studies of Reading

Three overarching types of activities were evident in the self-reports that we analyzed. First, a great deal of activity was in the service of constructing the meaning of the text. Some of this occurred before and some after reading, although the overwhelming majority of this activity occurred during reading (Levin & Pressley, 1981). Although there was more evidence of readers attempting to comprehend and learn from text than other processes, comprehension and learning were reported as regulated in part by *monitoring* activities. There was a great deal of evidence across the many self-reports that readers are aware of many different aspects of the reading process, with awareness affecting both strategies that were elected to cope with coming to understand text and evaluations that readers made of the text. In fact, readers' prior knowledge that could be related to text content was most apparent from reports of readers *evaluating* the text they were reading. Just as comprehension and monitoring are complex and multidimensional, so it is with evaluating. Many different types of evaluations stimulated by different characteristics of text were reported in the studies we reviewed. Finally, we found that the three activities of constructing meaning, monitoring, and evaluating were all influenced by the sociocultural context in which they occurred. The social nature of reading resonated throughout the accounts of these activities, despite the fact that the majority of studies did not have a specific focus on the social aspects of reading.

As we knew was the case from informal reading of the papers studied in our review, some studies were more complete in the processes they reported than others. The completeness of a report can be gauged roughly by the frequency of its mention in the results that follow. In particular, strategies, monitoring, and evaluation are each broken down into subclassifications. At the beginning of each presentation of subclassifications, the studies particularly contributing to the section are specified. Some studies are cited repeatedly, whereas others are mentioned only occasionally.

More often than not, the terms used to refer to a process varied from study to study. Different researchers working in the same area sometimes use different terms to refer to what we consider the same processes. The specific terms adopted here are ones that we believe best make the process represented transparent. Although we made great efforts to eliminate redundancies in processes specified, admittedly some overlap probably remains. Also, because there is dynamic interplay between meaning construction processes, monitoring, and evaluation (good reading demands this), it is somewhat reductionistic to attempt to isolate these activities. To describe them, however, isolation was necessary; for meaning making, monitoring, and evaluating were each manifested in many different ways in the self-reports. Thus, this chapter is divided into three sections, one devoted to meaning construction and learning processes, the second to monitoring, and the third to evaluating. For the most part, integration across these categories of reader activities is left until the concluding chapter, although there is some discussion in this chapter about how particular reading activities influence other activities. Each of the three sections are divided further into subsections, each of which begins with an outline of the activities included in it, followed by integrative commentary about the activities included in the outline.

Probably no reader does all of the activities covered in this chapter in reading any particular text, and we expect that reader activity varies with the purpose and goal of reading. Indeed, some of the activities preclude other ones (e.g., skimming and front-to-back careful reading are often incompatible). What is covered here are possible routes, alternatives that readers can and sometimes do elect. Our intent was to catalog the many options that the reader can consciously control during reading. Throughout the discussion, there are occasional references to studies other than think-aloud analyses when doing so permits placement of the findings in a larger context. We refer to other work when the rich descriptions of skilled reading permitted by think-alouds can be rendered richer by relating them to insights about reading produced using other paradigms.

IDENTIFYING AND LEARNING TEXT CONTENT

Regardless of a reader's goal—whether reading is done in preparation for a test, in anticipation of a writing assignment, with the expectation of sharing it in a conversation, to determine an author's perspective, or as part of staying abreast in an area of interest—it is necessary to identify the important information in a text. Not surprisingly, a large proportion of the comments included in think-alouds are directed at identifying the meaning in text. Although the think-aloud studies did include readers reading for a number of purposes, often study participants were reading to prepare for a test on the text content. Thus, the think-alouds we reviewed included many comments about processes intended to increase the memory of text.

The various activities reported by readers that comprise meaning identification, meaning construction, and coding of text meaning can be categorized into activities that occur before reading, during reading, and after reading. As we show, however, these are hardly discrete or independent stages. For example, overviewing affects careful reading of text; whether first reading of text results in understanding affects postreading processing of content. Nonetheless, the strategies reviewed in this section can be more easily outlined through discussion of activities before, during, and after reading than by focusing on connections between pre-, on-line-, and postprocessing of text. Thus, we continue with our examination of reading, taking a linear and individual tack on what we acknowledge to be a recursive and interactive activity.

Before Reading

Readers (good readers, at least, as many of the readers were in these studies) do not simply dive into a text, but rather try to size it up first, in particular, with respect to their goal in processing the text. These readers plan, a priori, how to approach the reading depending on the task demand, including the anticipated difficulty and length of the material. This often affects subsequent reading. In other cases, overviewing material results in a decision not to read the piece in question carefully, or only to skim it. In what follows, we emphasize both what readers can do and what they can learn from prereading activities[1]:

Prereading activities

1. **Constructing a goal for reading of this text (i.e., knowing what the reader wants to get out of the text).**
2. **Overviewing (skimming) the text**
   A. **Noting characteristics of the text, such as the length and structure**
   B. **Noting important parts, especially important information covered in the text**
   C. **Gathering information about what might be in the text that is relevant to the reading goal**
   D. **Determining what to read and in what order**
   E. **Determining what to read in detail**
   F. **Determining what to ignore**
3. **Deciding to read only particular sections and which particular sections (i.e., ones most likely to contain information of interest to the reader**

---

[1]Studies making major contribution to this list: Afflerbach (1990b), Charney (1993), Guthrie et al. (1991), Kintgen (1983), Lundeberg (1987), Schmalhofer & Boschert (1988), Shearer, Coballes-Vega, & Lundeberg (1993), and Wyatt et al. (1993).

or relevant to the reading goal), or to read particular sections before reading others (e.g., read the general sections first, such as the abstract, introduction, or conclusions of a scientific article)

4. **Deciding to quit** the reading because the content in the reading is not relevant to current reading goals

5. **Activating prior knowledge and related knowledge**
   A. Through **mental search** of what one knows about topic, the text structure, and author intention
   B. **Reading reference list** to activate prior knowledge

6. **Summarizing** what was gained from previewing

7. Based on overviewing, **generating an initial hypothesis about what the text is about**, one that can be revised or refined in light of information gained during subsequent and more careful reading

Good readers are saliently aware of their purposes as they begin to process a text (e.g., to inform one's program of research, the design of a particular study, to know what so-and-so is thinking these days), often knowing even before they read what they want to get out of the reading in question. Thus, mindfulness is a hallmark of the many subjects who have participated in verbal report studies. Readers use their knowledge of purpose to build a frame in which their efforts and resources can be used efficiently.

Awareness of reading goals directs the initial processing of text; that is how overviewing and skimming are carried out. In going through a text quickly, the reader is looking for what might be important parts, especially relative to the reading goal. These activities are carried out in anticipation of a more careful reading of the text. Sometimes this activity concludes with an explicit summary by the reader of what was learned during the overview. Although these are frequent and often helpful strategies, there are times when experts will "jump into" the reading of a text.

There are many recommendations in the literature beginning with Levin and Pressley (1981; see Pearson & Fielding, 1991, for a history of this idea) that readers should activate prior knowledge related to a new text before attempting to read it. Similarly, prior knowledge is generally seen as enhancing the interaction of reader and text. Such explicit activation of prior knowledge was not self-reported much in the think-aloud studies. We suspect, however, that prior knowledge of the topic of a text is stimulated by overviewing, with the prior knowledge activation so automatic that it occurs out of consciousness and thus, is not reflected in self-reports. The richer a readers' prior knowledge related to the text that is read, the more automatic the activation may be. Alternatively, it may be that readers do not relate a new reading to their prior knowledge as completely as they could, at least at the beginning of a reading, which would be consistent with observations that students may not comprehend fully the significance of information they encounter, because they do not relate new material to what they already know as fully as they might (e.g., Pressley, Wood et al., 1992). Whether or not readers explicitly activate prior knowledge before reading, much more extensive processing is observed once front-to-back reading of text begins, with prior knowledge more saliently represented in activities during reading than before reading.

During Reading

The many activities that occur during reading can be subcategorized as involving initial reading of text, assigning relative importance to information in text, making inferences, integrating different parts of text, and interpreting. Of course, these do not occur in a linear sequence but rather are interwoven and relate to one another. Nonetheless, we review these reading processes a subcategory at a time, because any attempt to discuss them in an interrelated fashion would result in incomplete coverage of some activities and much confusion.

Reading Text Initially from Front to Back: Salient Processes/Behaviors During Front-to-Back Reading[2]

1. **Generally front-to-back (i.e., linear) reading of text**
   A. **Nonselectively or**
   B. **Selectively (e.g., slowing down when important information is encountered)**
2. **Reading only some sections, ones believed to contain critical information based on prior knowledge about the writing structures used in the genre, author style, or overviewing (i.e., recognizing unneeded information)**
3. **Skimming (i.e., less complete than front-to-back reading cited in last point)**
   A. **May be reading only for the gist**
   B. **May involve some selectivity, reading more slowly when important information is encountered**
   C. **Skipped material sometimes assumed to be correct**
4. **If text is easy, read using automatic processes with few intentional, conscious strategies aimed at meaning construction. This reliance of**

---

[2]Studies making major contribution to this list: Afflerbach (1990a, 1990b), Bazerman (1985), Caron (1989), Charney (1993), Collins, Brown, & Larkin (1981), Deegan (1993), Earthman (1989, 1992), Goldman & Saul (1990), Graves & Frederiksen (1991), Guthrie et al. (1991), Haas & Flower (1988), Hare (1981), Johnston & Afflerbach (1985), Kintgen (1983), Kucan (1993), Lytle (1982), Olshavsky (1976–1977), Olson et al. (1981), Phillips (1988), Pritchard (1990a), Schmalhofer & Boschert (1988), Schwegler & Shamoon (1991), Shearer et al. (1993), Trabasso & Suh (1993), Wade, Trathen, & Schraw (1990), Wood & Zakaluk (1992), and Wyatt et al. (1993).

automatic processes continues until something goes wrong—for example, a feeling that important meaning is being missed or miscomprehended, or the interaction of reader and text is such that nonautomatic, but still effective, processing is called for. (See the discussion of monitoring and strategies in this chapter.)

5. Reading aloud; voicing what is otherwise subvocal speech

6. Repeating/restating text just read to hold in working memory (i.e., contemplate it)

   A. Sometimes because working memory is full or at capacity

   B. Sometimes because only partial understanding of text has been accomplished and reader needs to repeat the text to complete the model held in working memory

7. Repeating/restating a thought that occurred during reading

   A. To hold in working memory

   B. To "explain" something in the text (see discussion on inferences later)

   C. The goal as discriminated from a related, but incorrect goal (e.g., "I need to be looking for range of gestation, not average gestation"; Guthrie et al., 1991, p. 216)

8. Making notes

9. Pausing to reflect on text (and perhaps notes, if made)

10. Paraphrasing part of text (i.e., recounting narrative or message of text; e.g., Sofia is in jail, The mayor slaps Sofia; Graves & Frederiksen, 1991, p. 7)

11. Explicitly looking for related words, concepts, or ideas in text and using them to construct a main idea, gist, or summary

12. Looking for patterns in the text

13. Predicting/substantiating (i.e., draft-and-revision strategy for main ideas of text as well as how the author has structured the text)

    A. Hypothesizing a tentative interpretation (i.e., a text schema, image, or macrostructure) of overall paragraph/text meaning and/or tentative understanding of the structure of the paragraph/ text

       a. Sometimes only a partial understanding emerges from first reading, even a careful first reading

       b. Based on skimming of the passage

       c. Based on what is known about the topic, with more predictions likely in reactions to readings on a topic familiar to the reader

       d. Based on macrostructural cues (e.g., knowledge of structures of the genre, salient structural cues obvious during a skim)

  e. Based on what is known about key words, title, pictures, citations in the reference list

  f. Based on what is known about author, author's perceived intention and values

  g. Based on what has been read up until this point

B. Predicting content/structure based in part on the hypothesized interpretation/structure, with subsequent evaluations of predictions emanating from hypothesized interpretation/structure as more information is encountered in text

  a. Specific event/structure expected in reading

  b. Type of information that should be covered in this type of reading

C. Concluding previous hypothesis is valid/invalid based on subsequently encountered piece of information (e.g., specifically citing evidence for or against hypothesis)

D. Looking for information consistent/inconsistent with expectations (e.g., looking for expected parts of a writing, such as expected rhetorical structures in light of suppositions about the genre/structure of the piece)

E. Retrieving information thought about earlier for additional consideration when new information relevant to the idea under consideration is encountered

  a. Retrieving text read that was "on hold" in working memory or long-term memory

  b. Retrieving thought(s) made in reaction to earlier text

F. Adjusting a tentative expectation/interpretation immediately after generating it, recognizing after it is generated that it really is not consistent with all of the material presented up until this point

G. Adjusting initial ideas about text content based on newly encountered information in text, including information not consistent with expectations (e.g., rebinding, Collins et al. 1980; draft and revise, Johnston & Afflerbach, 1985)

  a. Hypotheses competing with initial hypothesis about text meaning are generated in reaction to particular words in the text, individual sentences, paragraphs, or the whole text; original hypothesis and new hypotheses are evaluated for viability as new information in text is encountered

  b. Macropropositions of text meaning constructed during overview and early reading are adjusted as confirmation and refutation of expectations occurs during reading; conducting a fine tuning of the model of text the reader is constructing

    c. Questioning of the default assumptions made when information in a text conflicts with hypothesized interpretation (e.g., questioning the assumptions typically made when reading, such as, "This text refers to events in the real world," "This is about a standard coffee can," "These are normal rocks"; Collins et al., 1980, p. 398)

  H. Maintaining an hypothesis: Not adjusting initial ideas based on new information encountered in text because new information is not considered credible

  I. Jumping back to reconsider previously read information in light of information encountered later in the text

  J. Generating several tentative hypotheses, holding them in working memory as possible interpretations, and evaluating the viability of them as new information in the text is encountered

14. Resetting reading/learning goals at a different level of understanding because the text suggests that there might be a more appropriate goal

Although readers do not always read straight through from the front to the end of a text, this is the general progression that reading follows. Because this reading often comes only after before-reading overviewing, readers, nonetheless, have some perspective on what the whole of the text might mean before the front-to-back processing begins. In some cases, much of the reading is really not strategic at all, involving automatic decoding of text and effortless comprehension of content (e.g., Johnston & Afflerbach, 1985). That is, much of the time the meaning of text is obvious from a single reading and consistent with expectations given the topic and what the reader knows about the topic based on previewing and prior knowledge. When that is the case, reading simply proceeds along at a rapid pace, and the information processing demand is quite manageable.

On other occasions, text is more challenging and/or unpredictable. One tactic for dealing with difficult texts is to pause and reflect on the meaning, as did one subject in Johnston and Afflerbach (1985): "And right now I'm just staring blankly at the page . . . trying to gather . . . probably not . . . well, I'm not reading anything new . . . and I think I'm just cycling these things around to see if anything seems reasonable" (Johnston & Afflerbach, 1985, p. 213). Another tactic for dealing with difficulty is to read aloud. Although the effects of this tactic are not clear, such reading does force more conscious attention and slower processing of text than typically occurs during silent reading. Perhaps the conscious nature of reading aloud is reassuring to the reader, as is the deliberate (and often manageable) rate of processing text. Another tactic is to shift focus away from currently difficult portions of the text (or ideas in the text) in favor of other, related sections (or related ideas), which if understood, might provide hints about the meaning of others parts of the passage or the passage as a whole. Thus, Phillips (1988) reported a student who was very confused about whether a story was about a restaurant or a picnic, until he decided to shift focus and resolve what type of "glasses" were being referenced in the reading. The student believed that if it could be determined whether drinking or field glasses were the referents, then it might be possible to determine whether the text was about a restaurant or a picnic.

The think-alouds were extremely revealing about the dynamics of comprehension difficulties and how understandings of text shift in reaction to comprehension difficulties and surprises in text. This process starts before reading begins: Both before reading and early in reading, hypotheses about the potential meaning of a text emerge, such as this prediction generated by one of Afflerbach's (1990b) subjects after reading the title of an essay on censorship: "This is gonna be . . . from what I know about this stuff . . . probably about how the-uh . . . textbook publishers are-are subject to so much pressure from special interest groups . . . uh . . . that the textbooks have gotten so watered down that they're not meaningful" (Afflerbach, 1990b, p. 142). One of Afflerbach's (1990a) subjects relied on phrases referring to well-known concepts to generate an initial hypothesis when reading the first sentence in a reading, reporting the following: "I'm identifying the words I really know, for example 'contemporary cultures in the northeast.' So that would be my first guiding point. So, OK, this, obviously this paragraph is going to talk to me about some kind of cultural study done in the northeast" (Afflerbach, 1990a, p. 42).

Predictions are stimulated by meaning cues (e.g., key words, key references, pictures), structure cues in text (e.g., structures flagging cause-and-effect relationships, such as phrases that include *because, resulting in, as a consequence of*), and cues about the intentions of the author or purpose of the text (e.g., the text is an editorial by a noted neo-conservative and the author's name evokes reader's knowledge and emotions related to previous encounters with the author's writing), in interaction with the reader's prior knowledge of the topic covered by the text and his or her knowledge of writing conventions. Depending on the theoretical framework of an investigator, various researchers refer to these overarching hypotheses about meaning that emerge as schemata (e.g., R. C. Anderson & Pearson, 1984), images (e.g., Rosenblatt, 1978), or macrostructures (e.g., van Dijk & Kintsch, 1983). To reduce confusion, we use macrostructures consistently to refer to such hypotheses in what follows.

Structure cues are sometimes more salient than meaning cues in stimulating hypotheses about what is likely to be in a text. Here is an example of a prediction emanating from structure cues: "OK . . . seems like I'm gonna get something about history here . . . usually . . . when I write or something . . . and I use that phrase 'is nothing new' I'm trying to set the reader up . . . to read about history . . . and also—my eye caught on the next sentence—'For nearly a century' " (Afflerbach, 1990b, p. 142). We also note that this expert reader demonstrates the ability to approach reading from the perspective of the writer. Familiarity with the conventions of writing allows expert readers to anticipate meaning as they draw on their experiences and familiarity with composition.

Haas and Flower (1988) presented another example of a reader generating an early hypothesis about a psychology text's structure: "It seems that different points are being brought out and each has a kind of contradiction in it, and it seems like an introduction . . ." (p. 173). Another student hypothesized in reaction to another part of the text, "Maybe he's (the author) contrasting the verbal glibness with caveman instinct" (p. 173).

In the early stages of reading a text, a macrostructure is only a hypothesis about meaning, and readers understand the tentativeness of early expectations about meaning. The earlier a reader is in a reading, the less definite the reader is about whether the current hypothesis is the meaning of the text. In fact, as reading proceeds, there is a continuous evaluation of whether the provisional macrostructure currently in place is consistent with information being encountered in the text. Sometimes a macrostructure will be generated only to be dismissed immediately when the reader recognizes that it is not consistent with all of the information encountered thus far in text. For example, Phillips (1988) reported a student who was reading a passage about farming. First, the student concluded that grain was being put in one place as it was cut; however, he then immediately reconsidered this conclusion. The reconsideration was based on recognition of an inconsistency between the placement of the grain and information in the text. Thus, the student decided that the grain was being placed elsewhere. Such shifts are sometimes quite obvious in the protocols, as when one of Afflerbach's (1990a) subjects remarked, "This is not what I thought the paragraph was about" (p. 42), as an initial hypothesis was rejected when information not congruent with it was encountered near the end of the paragraph.

To the extent that new information is consistent with expectations based on the current macrostructure, the macrostructure is preserved. To the extent that new information conflicts with expectations based on the current macroproduction, there is motivation to modify the macrostructure so that it is as consistent as possible with all of the information in the text. Phillips (1988) provided an example of such a modification as a student read a passage about fishing:

> After reading the first episode, the student thought that a group of sailors was heading out to sea. After the student read episode B, he questioned his previous interpretation by saying, "They're fishermen (not sailors like I thought), because it says here the net was hard to pull. Also, it says that they were catching fish." (p. 203)

Similarly, Afflerbach (1990b) reported how a reader came to meaning as reading proceeded:

> (Reads title: "Benefits of carpeting")
> I'm gonna learn to carpet something.

(Reads first sentence)
I just see that as a lead-in . . . and I'm expecting to find out what this is all about.
(Reads second sentence)
I'm not gonna learn about carpet . . . I'm gonna learn about the effects of carpeting in the classroom.
(Reads third sentence)
. . . I'm adjusting the scenario that I expect . . . a little . . . by-by expecting this to be an argument in favor of . . . why we ought to carpet perhaps. (p. 144)

Afflerbach (1990b) also reported a shift in a reader's report of the perceived author's purpose following processing of the first paragraph of a passage, in which a subtle shift in tone was detected:

Now that to me . . . sounds a little less . . . the way they phrased "enobling nature of sports and transformed it into a religion" leads me to believe that I'm gonna have to adjust my initial impression of this person . . . maybe he's going to say some things that aren't so wonderful about it. (p. 143)

It is not unusual for readers to have several alternative meaning possibilities in mind at the beginning of a text, which can be evaluated as more information is encountered, as in this example from Phillips (1988) as a student read a passage about skiing:

The student thought that the people were either skiing or tobogganing . . . [w]hen asked why Marty was scared a little, raised several alternatives: "Maybe he's going to do something . . . or learn some lesson . . . or do something he's never done before. Those are the things that come to mind. (pp. 203–204)

Although readers sometimes are conscious of inconsistencies between expectations and emerging interpretations of text, evaluations of consistency and shifts in interpretation often occur automatically. Even so, there are certainly occasions when sophisticated readers actively look for information in text that is informative about their expectations and tentative hypotheses about text content. There are also occasions when they actively construct new hypotheses about the meaning of text when it is clear that their current understanding is not consistent with the information now being encountered. Indeed, if the meaning encountered in the text is surprising enough, there may be a dramatic rethinking of one's assumptions, such as when it suddenly becomes apparent that some of the relationships specified in the text could not possibly occur in the real world and hence, this write-up, which had been assumed to be a factual report, must be science fiction. All of the hypothesis testing required to understand a text involves mental effort. As meaning becomes clearer, and hypothesis testing, thus, becomes less necessary, there is a decrease in the effort required to understand the text, expressed by one of Wade et al.'s (1990) subjects: "What I found in reading this is that I'm getting more familiar with the subject matter. It's getting a little easier

analogies?
metaphors?

to understand. Therefore, I can read a little faster. There's an accumulation of knowledge that's starting to build up . . ." (p. 160).

If a reader really gets stuck in attempting to understand a text, such as when they have little prior knowledge that can be related to the text, they may attempt to think of an analogy that might make the meaning clearer:

> Whew! . . . I'm trying to think of things that might better help me understand what he's talking about here . . . the only thing that comes to mind . . . is culture repressing the instincts of man . . . I thought of Freud . . . and *Civilization and Discontent* . . . and maybe the man's trying to make a similar argument . . . but not doing it as clearly as Freud, and Freud writes pretty complex. (Johnston & Afflerbach, 1985, p. 216)

Although reading is generally front-to-back, sometimes there are reasons to jump ahead; for example, if the reader believes some important point that needs to be understood at the moment is in subsequent text (e.g., based on memory from the overviewing of the text). On other occasions, it becomes apparent there is need to jump back (e.g., to cover more completely information that was read over quickly the first time, but that now is crucial to understand in order to understand current content). Wade et al. (1990) reported such jumping back as particularly prominent in the skilled reading they observed, consistent with analyses offered by Garner and her colleagues (e.g., Garner & Reis, 1981) that looking back when confused or in need of additional information is a sophisticated reading strategy. One of Wyatt et al.'s (1993) subjects manifested such sophistication, recognizing the need to review an earlier section of text in light of information encountered subsequently: "So now that I looked at the instruments they used, I'm gonna go back and look at the design a little bit more because I didn't really look very closely at the design or the instruction. So I went back" (p. 61).

One dramatic realization that can occur during reading is that one's goal in reading a particular text is inappropriate (i.e., it may be too lofty, unattainable, or off target), with the adjustment being to change goals. For example, suppose the reader begins a statistics text with the goal of understanding when and where to use a statistical test described in the text. During the course of the reading, it might become apparent to the reader that the goal of this reading really should be to prepare a set of crib notes specifying how to compute the statistic, its assumptions, the vagaries of its application as described in the text, and a statement about what can be inferred from the results of the statistical computation. That is, it became clear during the reading that without the crib notes, there would be no hope of the reader being able to use the statistic later. The goal can shift from reading the text to understand it to reading so that a set of notes can be prepared.

Sometimes it becomes apparent to a reader that he or she cannot figure out the meaning in a current text without seeking information in another text. In that case, the reader may look up a reference or otherwise seek outside information before proceeding. There are also occasions when readers give up on trying to determine the meaning of some section of text after not finding clues in the text that permit a clear interpretation. Good readers appear to know when to call it "quits," upon exhausting efforts, strategies, and patience. And although attributions for not attaining a goal may vary (e.g., "This author lacks talent," "This is horrible writing," "I'm not doing so well"), expert readers appear relatively unscathed by their unsuccessful (or only partially successful) encounters with text.

Alternatively, the reader can distort some of the information in the text in order to convince him or herself of the correctness of a tentative interpretation that is not really in syncrony with information in the text, as when one of Phillips (1988) subjects, reading a passage about fishing, concluded early that the word *bay* referred to the Canadian department store, The Bay, and distorted information in the passage to support that interpretation (e.g., claiming that *nets* referred to in the story might be used to catch baby fish in a decorative waterfall at the department store).

The processing of text is not always mentally all consuming, with readers distracted sometimes by thoughts of other events in their lives or because of boredom. Although there are many more indicators of engagement (i.e., most of the behaviors summarized in this results section) than disengagement, disengagement can be striking, to the point of physically falling asleep in the middle of a reading.

In summary, meaning emerges during readers' front-to-back, first reading of text. The reader shapes the clay of the text. Initial hypotheses about meaning are refined as information is encountered that is not included or not consistent with initial macrostructures. A number of tactics contribute to this process. In order to generate tentative hypotheses of text meaning, prior knowledge of the topic of the reading (or related topics) is necessary. A likely hypothesis is that good readers inhibit the generation of predictions and hypotheses about meaning when they monitor that they lack prior knowledge related to the topic of a text (e.g., Bruce & Rubin, 1984), a possibility consistent with some of the think-aloud data reported by Afflerbach (1990b) and Afflerbach and Johnston (1984), who observed more predictions when readers read in familiar topic areas. Indeed, Afflerbach observed readers consciously withholding predictions based on their awareness of lack of background knowledge as they read a passage used by Bartlett (1932). This is illustrated in the following example:

(Reads title: "War of the Ghosts")
Well . . . this could . . . could be anything.
(Reads first sentence)
This isn't helping me very much . . . I'm not exactly sure what to expect . . . from the title . . . I'm just going to take a wait-and-see attitude. (Afflerbach, 1990b, p. 143)

Another reader of the same story reported awareness of inability to predict in the middle of the "War" story: "This isn't familiar at all . . . the story doesn't make sense . . . thus far . . . I'm just reading sentence by sentence . . . they're not really linked too well . . . and you can't predict anything . . . it's unpredictable" (Afflerbach, 1990b, p. 143).

In contrast, there are also poor readers who do not monitor well when they do not know much about a topic and who generate tentative passage meanings without reflection. For example, Williams (1993) observed that learning-disabled readers often generate associations to words or phrases in readings, resulting in responses to reading and hypotheses about meaning that have little to do with the messages in the passage. Our reading of Williams' work is that there is little evidence, however, that the learning-disabled readers evaluate or refine their hypotheses about meaning as reading proceeds, emphasing that the outline of reading processes in this chapter is an outline of skilled reading.

But this is just the start of understanding how understanding develops during skilled reading. For example, there are many processes involved in the identification of main ideas that have not been discussed yet, but that were apparent in the think-alouds we reviewed.

More About Identifying Important Information in Text[3]

1. **Looking for information relevant to personal or professional goals or specific reading goals for this text (i.e., reading selectively)**
2. **Deciding which pieces of information in text are important (in relation to the goal involved in reading this text)**
    A. **Use prior knowledge of the text topic, text structure, author, and so on to decide what is important to attend during processing the text**
    B. **Use terms that one knows in a difficult text to determine what is important in the text and to construct meaning of the text**
3. **Looking specifically for what is "news" in the reading**
    A. **Go to sections most likely to contain news, skipping other sections to do so**
    B. **Especially attend to things that are surprising, not fitting expectations**
4. **Dismissing information presented in text because it is not consistent with prior knowledge (i.e., accepted thinking in the domain covered by the reading)**
5. **Looking for/acquiring key words**

---

[3]Studies making major contribution to this list: Afflerbach (1990a, 1990b), Bazerman (1985), Charney (1993), Fletcher (1986), Guthrie et al. (1991), Hare (1981), Johnston & Afflerbach (1985), Kintgen (1983), Lundeberg (1987), Lytle (1982), Shearer et al. (1993), Wade et al. (1990), Wood & Zakaluk (1992), Wyatt et al. (1993).

[handwritten margin note: doesn't this depend on genre & purpose? (def. protocols)]

A. Using concepts (words) that are repeated in a text in order to decide what is important in the text

B. Identifying domain-specific vocabulary in a reading

C. Copying key words, phrases

D. Noting qualifying words, such as *if, when, only*

6. Looking for topic sentences

7. Looking for topic paragraphs

8. Noting parts of text to remember for future reference

9. Noting references in the text that should be looked at or considered later

10. Highlighting, underlining, circling, making notes, outlining or somehow flagging important points in text, including important examples

11. Explicitly skipping examples because general points, which the reader is seeking, are not provided in examples

12. Copying key sentences

13. Adjusting importance ratings as additional text is encountered

A salient activity is to find the main ideas in the text and make certain that these ideas are remembered—or at least can be found again later if needed. The big ideas, of course, are always relative to the goals of the reader with respect to the text. That is, very different ideas may be considered main ideas if a reader is reading for one purpose versus another. Readers who have considerable prior knowledge about archeology who are reading a text on the dispersal of broadpoint arrowheads in New England may decide that the main idea is that (a) the archeological methods used by the researcher are acceptable; (b) cultural diffusion occurs at varied rates; (c) there are several plausible theories of how arrowheads were dispersed in New England; or (d) the author does not know what he is talking about (Afflerbach, 1990b).

The identification of main ideas is a dynamic process, again involving an interaction between readers' prior knowledge and characteristics of the text. Prior knowledge can affect the identification of main ideas in several ways:

[handwritten margin note: prior knowledge]

1. Prior knowledge can provide powerful hints about what might be included in this text that should be considered important (e.g., if one is writing a paper on civil rights violations in the South of the 1960s, prior knowledge might heighten sensitivity to names like George Wallace, Medgar Evers, or Lester Maddox).

2. Sometimes if the text is very difficult (e.g., because one's prior knowledge is low and hence, many terms in the text are foreign), one tactic for deciding what might be important is to focus on the parts of text that can be understood; for example, generating associations to parts of the text that are understood in

an attempt to construct the main ideas of the text. The quality of such associations, of course, depends on prior knowledge.

3. Even if all of the ideas in a text are comprehensible, not all are important.

The important ideas are often the new ones. Of course, to recognize the new ideas, one must know what the old ideas are. Obviously, those who are high in knowledge are more likely to separate the novel from the passé. In contrast, sometimes readers focus on the ideas in text that are more familiar (i.e., old ideas), with the result that these become the important parts of the text for them, as reflected in this think-aloud from Johnston and Afflerbach (1985): "Well, I do know something about spindle fibers . . . Okay . . . so they're looking at . . . actually . . . individual muscles" (p. 215). In summary, prior knowledge plays multiple, critical roles in determining whether and how readers identify main ideas in texts.

Individual words in texts can provide powerful hints about what is important. Readers are aware of this and report that they look for key words, ones sometimes flagged because they are obviously terms specific to the domain or are repeated in the text. Thus, one of Johnston and Afflerbach's (1985) subjects reported the following in noting repetition of the word *intellectual*: "In the first clause there . . . thinking about intellectual power . . . that ties back to the other things we talked about . . . the author's continual . . . or growing number of references to the guy as an intellectual" (p. 217). Other times, subjects note that concepts are repeated, even if exact words are not, such as when one of Johnston and Afflerbach's (1985) subjects decided on the main idea after noting the occurrence of *society, social,* and *cultural.* One reader in Wade et al. (1990) reported that key words were tremendously important throughout the processing of a passage in permitting identification, organization, comprehension, and memory of main ideas:

> I read through a section quickly. I try to figure out why it was put there and then I'll go back and underline as few words as possible that could describe the whole section. Then after each section I go back and read through everything I've highlighted up to this point. I write down the main ideas on 3×5 cards to consolidate it so that it's easier to study. Then I recite everything when it gets time to review it more. I go back and read it over again, looking at the key words and trying to remember the definitions for them. (p. 158)

Once main ideas are identified, readers consider it important to flag them. Sometimes mental notes are made about parts of text that are important. Other times physical marks and notes are made, including in some cases, copying the critical points into an external record. The use of physical marking systems is important for some students who are faced with learning the content of texts in preparation for an exam, permitting ready identification, long after reading, of points that should be attended to in carrying out a review, as one of Wade et al.'s (1990) subjects reported:

> When I have to review for a test, I will go back and look at my own underlinings and marginal notes. It's a fairly quick process and I feel I can remember what is most important to remember that way. Usually, when I go back and review, I find that these two types of marking form a kind of coherency in and of themselves—a whole chain of thought, which gives me what I need to have. I feel quite lost, usually, if I'm borrowing a book or an article from someone else and I don't dare put any marks in. I feel less confident in what I can remember. (p. 158)

I agree

Wade et al. (1990) reported on other subjects who combined underlining and construction of written summaries, with these permitting easy access to the big points in a text sometime after the text had been read originally.

Just as meaning construction is dynamic during a reading, shifting as new information is encountered, so is consideration of importance. Ideas considered important earlier can be dismissed if later text suggests they are not important. Ideas passed over the first time can be elevated in importance in light of text content making obvious their importance.

Thus far, the discussion has focused on ideas expressed directly in the text. Of course, readers frequently go beyond the information given in a text to understand and remember it, something recognized even in the earliest protocol analyses of skilled reading (e.g., Olshavsky, 1976–1977; Olson et al., 1981). Thus, we take up next the inferences readers make when they read.

Conscious Inference-Making[4]

1. **Inferring the referent of a pronoun**
   A. **Based on the most recent topic (i.e., of the last sentence)**
   B. **Exerting effort to do so when it is vague (e.g., ". . . on removing the fork the eye came with it"** [*fork* is the referent for *it*]**, Magliano & Graesser, 1993, p. 195; "Though slavery may at first seem inhuman, yet the traders have as much to plead in their own excuse, namely the advantages of *it*"** [*slavery* inferred as referent of *it*]**, Bereiter & Bird, 1985, p. 138)**

---

[4]**Studies making major contribution to this list: Beach (1972), Bereiter & Bird (1985), Caron (1989), Charney (1993), Christopherson, Schultz, & Waern (1981), Deegan (1993), Earthman (1989, 1992), Fletcher (1986), Haas & Flower (1988), Kintgen (1983), Kucan (1993), Lytle (1982), Magliano & Graesser (1993), Olshavsky (1976–1977), Olson et al. (1981), Pritchard (1990a), Rogers (1991), Schmalhofer & Boschert (1988), Shearer et al. (1993), Squire (1964), Trabasso & Suh (1993), Wade et al. (1990), Waern (1988), Wineberg (1991), Wood & Zakaluk (1992), Wyatt et al. (1993).**

2. Filling in deleted information (e.g., deleted punctuation in order to understand a dialogue; "They must have dropped it from the bridge earlier," Christopherson et al., 1981, p. 576)

3. Inferring the meanings of words based on internal (e.g., root words) and external context clues

4. Inferring the connotations of words and sentences in the text, not just their literal meanings

5. Relating information encountered in text to prior knowledge, from associations to wholistic themes of the entire text to focussed associations to very specific points made in the text

   A. Constructing explanations of what is in the text (e.g., explaining an event occurring in the text using prior knowledge)

   B. Generating examples of concepts covered in the text

   C. Generating elaborations of specific ideas in the text based on knowledge of the text, author, subject area

   D. Speculating beyond the information presented in the text

   E. Relating known ideas to new information in the text

   F. Relating events, objects, setting, words, phrases, and so on in current text to ideas in other texts, tales, legends, and so on

   G. Relating this content to important themes in a field/profession.

   H. Relating text content to personally important prior knowledge (e.g., one's own theories, writings, personal knowledge of the writer, important personal experiences)

   I. Relating text content to one's work/life

      a. Whether claims in text apply in one's own world (e.g., "For my students, I think I would have to teach them that"; Shearer et al., 1993)

      b. How ideas in text can/might be applied in one's own world

   J. Construction of an idea not contained in the text by combining the ideas in the text with prior knowledge of the topic covered by the text

   K. Relating point currently encountered in text to information presented earlier in text to explain it (i.e., constructing bridging inferences)

   L. Constructing an analogy to another situation to explain a point in text

6. Making inferences about the author

   A. Author's purposes, intentions, goals (e.g., "So the author is trying to make the argument that you need specialists in psychology";

Haas & Flower, 1988, p. 176; "This article is crying out for a new type of scientist or something"; Haas & Flower, 1988, p. 177)

   a. Effects intended on reader/actual effects on readers
   b. Intended audiences
   c. Social context in which the text was written, for example, the relationship of the author to the intended readers

B. Author's assumptions, world views, beliefs, motives—as well as other characteristics such as his or her class, background, and so on—or even the identity of the author (e.g., "I wonder if the article is from *Ms?*"; Haas & Flower, 1988, p. 176)

C. Author's sources

D. Author's strategies in constructing the text (e.g., "I wonder if they expected it to be so confusing"; Haas & Flower, 1988, p. 176)

E. Author's expertise in content area

7. Making inferences about the state of the speakers or actors in a text or the state of the world depicted in the text

   A. Speaker's/actor's intent
   B. Speaker's/actor's characteristics, backgrounds (e.g., emotions, socio-economic status)
   C. Inferring the state of the world from actions stated in text
   D. Inferring actions to accomplish goal or general action stated in text
   E. Inferring the instrument used to accomplish an action (e.g., inferring that a person *fishing* is using a *rod-and-reel*, Magliano & Graesser, 1993, p. 195)
   F. Instantiation of a noun category (e.g., reads "breakfast" and thinks "bacon and eggs"; Magliano & Graesser, 1993, p. 195)

8. Confirming/disconfirming an inference with information in subsequent text

9. Stating/drawing of/deducing implied conclusion

Many inferences are made by readers automatically and out of consciousness. In fact, skilled reading requires such inference making. Yet readers' think-alouds also contain many reports of inference making that involve conscious reflection. These inferences vary in scope, from inferences about word meanings to overall conclusions.

A number of types of information can be considered during inference construction, such as the use of both clues internal to a work and external to it, such as in this example reported by Waern (1988):

Exinanition? Queer word . . . . Ex, that means out or out of . . . Inan, I don't know what that means . . . So it must be something which is opposite to being a thoroughly philosophical thinker since it says: He was, in fact, a throughly philosophical thinker . . . this is the only thing possible to get out of this, I think (p. 342).

Readers often make inferences to fill in meaning gaps in text. Sometimes gaps are created intentionally by an author who wants readers to come to conclusions through implication (e.g., an author who builds a character through actions that imply certain traits). Rogers (1991) reported how one ninth-grade reader inferred characteristics of a character in a story as well as attributes of the setting in which the character existed:

> She (Emily) has something she doesn't want people to know. It's just like that secret or something and I don't think people should be pressuring her that much . . . I don't feel sorry for her the way the town does—they sort of feel pity for her because she's such an out-of-it type person, but no one is helping her be like the rest of the people in the town. I feel sorry for her because the town is like that. (p. 412)

Another reader made a similar inference about Emily: "She represents old fashioned ideas and how being strict kills her and the new ideas . . ." (p. 414). In other cases, the text is rich with implications because of the topic (e.g., implications about American youth in an article about radicalism in the 1960s) or the author's style (e.g., implications about propriety that follow from William F. Buckley's style, or Molly Ivin's style). On still other occasions, inferences are necessary because of poor writing, such as when a reader must make some effort to infer the referent of a pronoun.

Interactions between prior knowledge and text are salient in the case of making inferences, just as they were with respect to identification of main ideas. Thus, one of Wyatt et al.'s (1993) subjects reacted to data in an article in light of what he knew about desirable characteristics of scientific data and measurement in the domain of the article:

> And I'm looking at the scores on the prior knowledge test. And you'll notice they're fairly high. It's 13 out of a possible 15. So, you know, you wonder: What did this really measure? Looks like it kind of topped out. . . . I'm wondering to myself why they would do this—these guys are some fairly good researchers—why they're using this instrument. (p. 62)

The ability to generate examples of concepts covered in a text depends on prior knowledge, as do most other elaborations about the content of text. Thus, one of Wade et al.'s (1990, p. 161) subjects was able to relate personal knowledge of Panama's Atlantic and Pacific beaches to an explanation in a text of Atlantic and Pacific tides in order to understand a concept about tides being covered in the text. Implications that an author builds in a text often can only be realized by readers who possess relevant prior knowledge.

The sources of prior knowledge that feed into the implication process are diverse. They include general knowledge of the world, in-depth knowledge of specific fields, author intentions, memories from previously read texts, and in some cases, knowledge of an author's style and ideas through personal acquaintance with an author's work. For example, here is how one of Wineberg's (1991) historians responded to an idea he encountered while reading a letter from the colonial period pertaining to the Battle of Lexington: "What I think of is a book I read by Jack Rakove talking about how one of the problems at the time was getting the colonies to hang together, and to try to get some unity. So the 'refusing with her sister colonies' is kind of an appeal to the other groups" (p. 498). Wineberg's analysis of this remark is that the historian made associations and inferences well beyond what was contained in the text read, recognizing how the letter reflected the discord of the time, how the letter was not just commenting on a squabble among farmers and soldiers, which is how it is written, but a clash between the colonies and the King of England.

Readers also make inferences about the intentions of the author of the piece being read, what Wineberg (1991) referred to as the subtext. This can be accomplished in part by relating a document to the social context in which it was written and offered originally. For example, another historian reading the same letter about Lexington made the following inferences about the purpose of the author:

> It's a way to try and get people in England to see things their way; it's encouraging loyalty to the king but it's saying the government has messed up. It clearly shows that the Regular troops are guilty of the violence at Lexington. . . . It's not just a recapitulation of events, but it in fact frames events in terms of . . . the relationship of the crown to its government, and these are two different things. (Wineberg, 1991, p. 499)

Sometimes prior knowledge permits inferences that result in the construction of a rich biography of the author of a text, such as when one of Wineberg's historians read a piece written by Ezra Stiles, the President of Yale in 1775:

> Ezra Stiles for all his supposed democracy comes across as very kind of classist in a way. I mean, you can tell that Pitcairn is from the same class as Stiles. Maybe not, but they both are men of integrity because of their upbringing, so he's "a good man in a bad cause." And I get that sense from some of the terms that Stiles uses—I don't know what Stiles' background is but I assume he's not aristocratic but he's educated, probably a man of the cloth if he was president of Yale in the late 18th-century; at that point probably most of them were clergy. So he was educated even if not a noble. But Pitcairn probably was, because until World War II, I believe, most British commanders were, or its officers were, from nobility of some sort. (Wineberg, 1991, pp. 506–507)

Once inferences are made, sometimes readers are so definite about them that they explicitly state them in their think-alouds and presumably, would explicitly think the inference to themselves if they were reading without the thinking-aloud requirement being imposed. In other cases, the inferences are tentative. That is, they have the status of hypotheses, which are either confirmed or disconfirmed by subsequent text (i.e., the predicting–substantiating process described earlier occurs). The conscious reporting of inferences makes salient the constructivist nature of reading.

In our experience, it appears that expert readers reading in areas of their expertise (e.g., an historian reading history) are quite ego involved, to the point that their reports of inference making (and asides to the prior knowledge that is fueling the inferencing process) may become exaggerated. Making inferences is an area where expert readers may be disclosing strategies as much as they are "proving" their expertise.

The complicated nature of meaning construction during reading can be appreciated further by considering inferences involving disparate parts of text, which is taken up next. That is, there is more to meaning construction than even the many processes considered thus far. The processing revealed by think-alouds during reading is very, very complicated.

ego involvement (margin note)

Integrating Different Parts of Text[5]

1. Explicitly attempting to get the "big picture" of the meaning before worrying about how details are organized

2. Generating the big idea of the meaning of text as well as the development of ideas about component parts, with these related to one another during the reading of the text (e.g., "We have a mini-narrative within the larger text"; Graves & Frederiksen, 1991, p. 7) and affecting construction of each other: That is, the hypothesized macrostructure affects interpretations of components, as interpretations of components feed back and can confirm or disconfirm the macrostructure (and hence, increase confidence in the macrostructure or cause it to change).

   A. Inferring a macrostructure from specific points made in the text

   B. Explicitly use the hypothesized macrostructure to decide what points in a text mean

   C. When meaning of specific points clash with overall understanding:

      a. Consider changing the overall meaning that is emerging

      b. Reconsider whether a specific point may have been misunderstood

      c. Reserve judgment about the viability of (an) interpretation(s) until additional text is processed

? macrostructure (margin note)

[5]Studies making major contribution to this list: Afflerbach (1990b), Beach (1972), Bereiter & Bird (1985), Charney (1993), Collins et al. (1980), Deegan (1993), Earthman (1989, 1992), Goldman & Saul (1990), Graves & Frederiksen (1991), Guthrie et al. (1991), Haas & Flower (1988), Johnston & Afflerbach (1985), Kintgen (1983), Kucan (1993), Lytle (1982), Magliano & Graesser (1993), Olson et al. (1981), Pritchard (1990a), Shearer et al. (1993), Wade et al. (1990), Wood & Zakaluk (1992), Wyatt et al. (1993).

    D. Generating questions about specific points relating to the hypothesized macrostructure that the reader then attempts to answer (e.g., "Where were they?" "Why did the man plunk down $5?" "Who was the 'she' who tried to give him $2.50?"; Collins et al., 1980)

    E. Generating superordinate goal that subsumes actions in text (e.g., person eating breakfast as part of overall goal of getting to work; Magliano & Graesser, 1993, p. 195)

3. Noting different parts of text (e.g., intro, examples, final point) and their interrelationships (e.g., "I guess these are just examples," "Is this the introduction?" "This seems to be the final point"; Haas & Flower, 1988, p. 175)

    A. Story grammar elements for narratives

    B. Expository elements (e.g., cause-and-effect structures, compare-and-contrast structures)

    C. Noting how particular parts of the text contribute to overall meaning

        a. Recognizing coherence (or lack of it) between different parts of text (e.g., point just encountered in text revolves previous problems of comprehension)

        b. Noting logical relationships, such as cause and effect

        c. Generating connections between main parts of text if not obvious at first

4. Holding representations of the ideas developed in text in working memory (i.e., different pieces of information picked up from the reading), thinking about them in an attempt to generate an integration (Note: The resulting integrated idea requires less working memory to maintain in consciousness than the ideas leading up to it.) May involve explicitly stopping reading in order to reflect and generate summary

5. Combining text structure and contextual clues to determine the meaning in the text

    A. Using "relational" terms in order to decide what is important in the text and to organize ideas (e.g., second paragraph begins with "Later," so figure that in the first paragraph he is talking about something that occurred earlier)

    B. Using knowledge about how paragraphs are supposed to be related to one another in order to assist meaning inferences across paragraphs

    C. Using knowledge of paragraph structure in order to understand a specific paragraph (e.g., "I don't know what he's talking about here, but he's categorizing things . . . so I figure . . . Well, there are some categories to be looked at"; Johnston & Afflerbach, 1985, p. 218)

    D. Using knowledge of usual structure and content of the genre being read in order to understand the meaning of text (i.e., attempting to fit new information into the type of text structure the reader believes he or she is processing, such as looking for causes and effects when reader believes he or she is processing a cause-and-effect exposition)

6. Looking elsewhere in the text for information related to a point currently being encountered in the text (i.e., gathering information)

    A. In a table, figure, or the citation list

    B. Jumping forward to look for particular information (e.g., based on overview, reader believes that subsequent text includes something that would assist interpretation of information presented early in the reading)

    C. Jumping backward to look for particular information (e.g., to information not processed fully previously but that must be fully understood in order to understand a part of text now encountered)

    D. Going back and forth in text to detect similarities, differences, and points of contact between various sections of the text

7. Searching through the text after a first reading, hoping to find/stimulate a macrostructure that can account for all of the content and relations specified in the text, because a satisfactory one was not detected during first reading

8. Rereading text to search for intersentential connections

9. Relating the currently read text to a previous portion of text (e.g., one sentence to another, a clause to its entire sentence, a clause of a sentence to overall meaning of the text)

    A. To make sense of current text

    B. When a concept is developed in different parts of a text

    C. Examples that can be related to other parts of text

    D. Consistencies/inconsistencies across different parts of text

    E. Reviewing a term or point made earlier in a text because subsequent text makes clear that it is more important than the reader assumed when the term or point was first encountered

10. Making notes to assist/stimulate integration

    A. Listing important points in text (written or mental)

    B. Outlining (written or mental)

    C. Diagramming

automatic processes not articulated

As with all inferences, some integrations across various parts of text are automatic. Others occur only with reflection, and it is those that are captured by the think-aloud protocols. Prior knowledge about how texts are constructed and how text constructions are flagged plays a large role in integration across texts. For example, particular types of information are expected in particular parts of text, with these expectations playing a large role in how the text is processed. Thus, when review of some particular type of information is required in order to construct a complete understanding of text, readers know where to look.

Across-text integrations can involve both mental and physical actions and manipulations. Readers report that they do reflect on how pieces of information across text fit together, that they juggle various pieces of meaning to create a larger meaning. The physical actions range from simply turning backward or forward in a text to making external notes and outlines. For example, here is an example of reflection on and shuffling of ideas after the reader realizes that the word *remoteness*, encountered several sentences back, is important to understanding the text:

reflection on shuffling of ideas

> I guess so far . . . from these sentences . . . I'd say this guy's [the author] just trying to say what sets this guy [Haydon] apart . . . a little bit filling in that first sentence about "remoteness" from the other artists . . . here's a guy who's a painter who doesn't really hang out with painters . . . or stay in touch with them very much . . . and apparently . . . even with what you might call the institutional painting society . . . or whatever . . . basically just shuffling the sentences that I've already read here . . . uh . . . taking this guy at his word . . . that this is what the guy is about . . . that his subject is about . . . and building sort of . . . going back to the first sentence, the guy says what he's . . . he says something about "remoteness" . . . so you go through and look for this guy's proofs of "remoteness." (Johnston & Afflerbach, 1985, p. 216)

Wade et al. (1990) reported that some of the readers they studied tended to do a great deal of shuffling in the head in an attempt to integrate parts of text, such as in the following self-report provided by a reader about his general approach to reading:

> I guess I mentally picture the information. I have a mental model that I just apply this information to. I've always had a good memory. I rely on it. That's why I don't underline or mark anything. If it fits in, then it's going to stay in my memory. If it doesn't, it's useless information. It's like a model made out of Lego blocks. Each piece of information from the text put together is like a buildup of all these Legos. If it happens to fit because it is the same color or the right size, then it will fit in the model and stay there. Otherwise, you just chuck it out. So, I'm sticking blocks in my mental model. (p. 161)

Information in many parts of text contribute to the construction of overall meaning (e.g., the main idea of a passage, its macrostructure). This is apparent

macrostructure - overall emergent meaning

in the commentaries readers make about integration. Thus, after reading about the types of people living in the East side of a city and those living in the West, one of Bereiter and Bird's (1985) readers concluded, "So the East is upper class and the West is lower class."

The great need readers feel to construct a macrostructure is reflected in the integrative actions reported during thinking aloud. The jumping around in text, construction of external notes, and generation of questions about the text are all indicative of effort expenditure to understand a text. Indeed, when readers have not found a satisfactory overall interpretation after a first reading, they return to the text and search for additional information that might stimulate a macrostructure consistent with the claims in the text.

Just as macrostructures are the results of integrative activities, they affect how other information in a text is interpreted. That is, the hypothesized macrostructure is a powerful contextual determinant of the meaning of specific information encountered in text after the macrostructural hypothesis is formulated. Early meaning integrative activities affect subsequent integrations.

Up until this point, we have referred to the emergent meaning generally, with our preference for the term *macrostructure* implying that we believe that overall meaning of text is abstract. Although it probably is, there are a variety of representations (and cognitive activities producing representations) that readers report as part of construction of overall text meaning. Next, we turn to these representations and examine how they provide an additional window on the complexities reported as occurring as part of attempting to construct meaning and memories from text.

Interpreting[6]

1. **Paraphrasing parts of text into more familiar terms (e.g., "So we're talking about psychological principles here"; Haas & Flower, 1988, p. 175)**

2. **Visualizing concepts, relations, emotions specified in (inferrable from) a text**

3. **Identifying "symbols" or "symbolic language" and translating the meaning of the symbols**

4. **Instantiating prior knowledge schemata that are activated by information in the text (e.g., thinking about a particular restaurant while reading an article about the social hierarchies in restaurants)**

make real

---

[6]Studies making major contribution to this list: Beach (1972), Bereiter & Bird (1985), Deegan (1993), Earthman (1989, 1992), Haas & Flower (1988), Kintgen (1983), Kucan (1993), Lundeberg (1987), Lytle (1982), Pritchard (1990a), Schmalhofer & Boschert (1988), Schwegler & Shamoon (1991), Shearer et al. (1993), Squire (1964), Wade et al. (1990), Waern (1988), Wineberg (1991), Wyatt et al. (1993).

5. Empathizing with messages in text (e.g., empathizing with characters in a story)

6. Making claims about "what the author really wanted to say" instead of what he or she actually said

7. Constructing interpretive conclusions

 A. Based on when the writing was produced

 B. Based on author's perceived purposes and goals (e.g., concluding that author made arguments in a particular way so they would be acceptable to scientific community)

 C. Thinking about content after reading in order to come to conclusions about the messages in the text

 D. Thematic generalizations ("And I think that's the theme: The old generation versus the new generation"), sometimes by summarizing over several points in the text and sometimes based on as little as a single clause, phrase, or word

 E. Generalization about the mood, atmosphere, tone portrayed in the writing

 F. Inducing a generalization based on examples (either one example or a series of examples)

8. Constructing interpretive categorizations

 A. Of entire text type ("a structural-functionalist perspective on sexual identity," "a political appeal"), tantamount to a wholistic interpretation of the text in some instances

 B. Of parts of the text (e.g., a fiercely animated dialogue, with this character prosecuting and the other defending; there's the cause and here's the effect)

 C. Categorizing actions in text as instances of more general concepts (e.g., racism, sexism)

 D. Inferring a categorical macroproposition explaining several points made in the text (e.g., Based on the details of Smalltown and Tinyville, I infer that Smalltown is on the better side of the tracks, and the residents of Tinyville are very much dependent on charity from Smalltown)

9. Physically or mentally doing (enacting) what the text instructs the reader to do (or suggests people should do) and then confirming the expected outcome or noting the discrepancy from the expected

10. Constructing (and/or holding in memory) alternative interpretations of what is going on in story (perhaps ones at different levels, such as more concrete versus more abstract/universal)

11. Constructing (and/or holding in memory) alternative perspectives on a story from the perspectives of different characters in the tale

12. Pretending to deliberate with others while reading the text, perhaps by talking to themselves, with alternative interpretations entering the dialogue

Readers report constructing many different types of representations of text meaning and engaging in a number of interpretive processes as they read. Some of the interpretations involve making text more concrete, such as the instantiation of schemata and the generation of visual images. Concretization does not imply simplicity, however, for images can be quite complex. Consider the image reported by one of Wade et al.'s (1990) subjects, and the rich prior knowledge that the reader calls on to construct the image:

> I tried to put in my mind visual pictures of tides rising, ebbing. Picturing the things that the author is saying about the strait, how the waters come together in the opposing forces of the different tides, what happens to the fish. Putting myself on the different beaches that they were talking about—trying to relate the ideas that they were talking about with personal experiences that I've had in order to make the ideas seem more realistic. (p. 161)

Other representations are inductions of generalizations from specific elements mentioned in the text, including the generation of themes, moods, and categories of events (e.g., "It's about how we need friends . . . how we have to work at keeping them . . . and how we have to learn to understand them"; Waern, 1988). Most interpretations are generated covertly, although a few can be overt, such as acting out the directions provided in text and dialoguing about possible alternative meanings of the text. Every reader who attempted any one of the interpretational activities considered in this section, even with respect to the very same text, would produce a somewhat different representation (i.e., different readers have different envisionments of the Grinch's Whoville, different empathetic reactions to Oliver in *Love Story*, and different instantiations of *A Streetcar Named Desire*). That is, interpretive reading is creative.

The dependence of readers on prior knowledge in constructing interpretations of text comes through in all of these representational/interpretational activities. The images, instances, and categories that occur reflect readers' prior knowledge. Empathetic reactions to fictional characters depends in part on experiencing empathy in real life; recognizing mood and atmosphere as depicted in text is affected by mood and atmosphere experiences in real life. The long-term content of the reader's mind comes through as they think aloud during reading, with what is active in their short-term memory—and hence available for self-report—being a product of messages in the text and the portions of long-term knowledge stimulated by the messages in the text.

One interesting approach to reading text is to construct an internal dialogue over the meaning of the text, attempting in one's own mind to engage in the discussion the reader believes the author in the text was attempting to stimulate. Wineberg's (1991) historians provided examples of this, for example, generating dialogue between the historian's vision of a prototypical reader during the colonial period responding to the imagined intentions of the author of a text depicting the Battle of Lexington, intentions that the historian relates as half of a dialogue between the envisioned reader and author. Much reading between the lines occurs during such an exercise. Thus, "hostilities are already commenced in the colony by the troops under the command of General Gage," is related as, "I mean here is who really started the hostilities. It's a way of telling, you know, we are loyal fellow subjects, but, you know, look what's happened under this ministry" (Wineberg, 1991, p. 505). The phrase, "for refusing, with her sister colonies" is translated, "Note, 'we're not alone in this fellows' (laughter)" (p. 505). During self-generated dialogues, readers can infer both the intentions of authors and how text was received by intended audiences.

As diverse as the interpretations considered in this section are, they do not exhaust the ways that readers react to text content. Later in this chapter, we take up the many types of evaluations readers make in reaction to text. For now, however, identifying and learning what is in text continues after a first reading is completed and thus, our attention now turns to what goes on after a reader makes it through the text the first time.

After Reading[7]

1. **Rereading after the first reading**
   A. **Linearly and nonselectively or**
   B. **With an eye out for particular information**
   C. **Skimming**
2. **Recitation of text to increase memory of it**
3. **Listing pieces of information in text**
4. **Constructing cohesive summary of the text**
5. **Self-questioning, self-testing over text content**
6. **Imagining how hypothetical situations might be viewed in light of information in text**
7. **Reflecting on information in article, with possibility of this reflection going on for a very long time and consequent shifts in interpretation unfolding over an extended period of time**
8. **Rereading parts of text following reflection in order to reconsider what is in text exactly in light of insights gained during reflection**

---

[7]**Studies making major contribution to this list: Bazerman (1985), Charney (1993), Deegan (1993), Earthman (1989, 1992), Goldman & Saul (1990), Kintgen (1983), Lundeberg (1987), Shearer et al. (1993), Wade et al. (1990), Wyatt et al. (1993).**

9. **Continually evaluating and possibly reconstructing an understanding of the text**

10. **Changing one's response to a text as the understanding is reconstructed**

11. **Reflecting on/mentally recoding text in anticipation of using it later (e.g., participating in a discussion of the text; Kintgen, 1983)**

After going through a text once, there can either be mental review, for example, through recitation or self-testing, or physical review through rereading. Rereading can result in information not noted as important previously being attended to more carefully. Some readers, especially if they are reading text in preparation for an examination, have great faith in rereading, with their articulated use of strategies boiling down to sophisticated rereading, such as was reported by this student in Wade et al. (1990):

> I skim through the reading, and then I go back and reread it more slowly, searching for important points that stand out and highlighting those. Then, I read it through again . . . I read it a couple of times, and when I come across a point I think is important, I slow down and study that information and reread it a couple of times. (p. 159)

Recitation involves paraphrasing, which necessarily involves selection and interpretation. Self-questioning is known to increase meaningful processing of text (e.g., Wong & Jones, 1982), with the result that the text is more completely understood, with it especially likely that self-questioning increases reader associations between text content and prior knowledge (Pressley, Wood et al., 1992). At least some active readers report self-questioning extensively as they attempt to learn from text, as exemplified by two example self-reports provided by Wade et al. (1990):

> So I ask myself questions and then study what I need to remember about tides, or what they do, when they happen, where different things occur. Just a who, what, when, why question . . . I'm thinking about the test that will follow and what kinds of questions will be asked. To be able to answer questions at the end, I need to know how tides work. If the questions aren't too specific, I'll be able to answer them. So, the information I'm gathering is to make a whole picture instead of just little bits of information that you can't remember because they don't tie into anything. (p. 161)

> . . . I go back and ask myself questions. I read a couple of sentences. Then I kind of quiz myself. What is this about? What am I reading? Could I reiterate this when I talk about it? (p. 161)

Although most of the post-reading processing reported in the think-aloud literature occurs immediately after reading, there have been occasional reports of reflection, review, and modification of thinking about text long after a text has been read. This is probably because most think-aloud studies have not collected long-term data, which is unfortunate, for long-term processing and use of text is definitely important. We cannot determine what occurs in the continuing interaction of reader and the understood text after the actual reading is completed. It is probable that the reader engages in internal dialog, modifying existing schemata in reaction to some new information, dismissing other information that is determined to be unnecessary, innaccurate, or uninteresting.

Summary

Identifying and learning the content of text involves processing before, during, and after first reading (Levin & Pressley, 1981), with continuous interaction occurring during the process. Thus, ideas about text that are formulated during overview can influence expectations about meaning and reading behaviors in pursuit of meaning (e.g., looking ahead during reading because the overview suggests that there is something late in the reading that might increase under-standing the part of text being processed at that moment). Whatever the beginning expectations about the meaning of a text, these are modified as the information in text is encountered during the first reading. Expectations that are confirmed are stablized in the emerging macrostructure; those that are disconfirmed are eliminated or changed. At the end of a reading, the reader may not be completely satisfied that he or she yet comprehends the text completely, leading to additional processing, such as rereading. Even if the meaning seems clear, the reader may take some actions to increase memory of it, such as rehearsing it or asking questions about the text, queries intended to deepen understanding of the sig-nificance of the content.

There is elegant coordination of processes as effective readers go through text, with the dynamics of such articulations sometimes captured in think-aloud pro-tocols, including shifts in strategies as the text meaning and content becomes clearer. Consider this sample from a participant in Wade et al.'s (1990) study, a student reading a passage in anticipation of a quiz on it:

> I stopped and read it very, very slowly and then tried to develop what I thought was the meaning. Then I wrote it down as a question and looked for the answer. I underlined the first half, which was already explained in prior sections. Then I circled the second part of it because that was the point they were going after—the main topic. That's what I think they're going to discuss next. Then I wrote down examples that support the main idea here and circled it once again. . . .
>
> My approach is changing. I think the text is getting a little easier to read. I was thinking, hey, this all fits together. I'm looking for topic sentences—for structure indicators. I should have used them earlier. I can see the topic in this section and supporting information, which are good examples. Then another topic sentence,

which supports the first one. . . . But the structure so far wouldn't mean anything unless I went back and envisioned it—I'm trying to picture the structures in my head. I circle what I think is a main idea. Then I underline supporting details. Here I numbered them—1, 2, 3, 4 reasons or causes. . . . In this section, I drew lines between the relationships to connect them together. For example, this says that tidal friction is gradually slowing down the rotation of the earth. Well, that's a cause-and-effect relationship. Then, on the next page, it said that tidal friction will be exerting a second effect. I realized that was an important thing. The author was listing something. That was the thing that clued me into coming back and making sure I had that as an arrow. . . . In this section I did a lot of note-taking in the margins. I summarized points, both main and supporting. Had it been written very clearly and concisely, I would have underlined it. But, because it was expressed in quite a few sentences and with a lot of examples, I summarized instead of underlining. (pp. 197–198)

Although the behaviors that readers exhibit in pursuit of meaning are diverse, they are coherent and sensible in light of what is known about human information processing. Consider the following examples:

1. The expectations about content formed before reading are akin to expectations formed at the outset of many tasks, expectations that guide processing as they are shifted as a result of processing (e.g., Miller, Galanter, & Pribram, 1960).

2. Both automatic and effortful processes typify many different tasks (e.g., J. R. Anderson, 1990), with both types of processes reported by readers in the studies informing this chapter. Given that verbal protocols reveal conscious processing (Ericsson & Simon, 1984/1993), it should not be surprising that readers in the self-report studies reported much more about their nonautomatic processing of text relative to automatic processing.

3. Humans typically "go beyond the information given" (Bruner, 1973), so that the many ways inferences and integrations are made should not be surprising. Although many of the inferences studied by psychologists are made automatically (e.g., see Graesser & Bower, 1990), what our review makes clear is that readers expend a great deal of conscious effort in pursuit of integrated understanding of text. Capable readers understand that going beyond the information given is what is required to get meaning from text.

4. Human representations of knowledge are diverse, including associations, images, hierarchical relationships, and schemata (see Pressley with McCormick, 1995, chapter 3). Thus, readers reported consciously attempting to construct diverse representations. The type of representation a reader generates seems to depend greatly on the type of information in the text that is being processed.

5. As readers go beyond the information given to construct representations of text content, they create unique understandings, unique interpretations. Consistent with various frameworks, from schema (e.g., R. C. Anderson & Pearson, 1984) to reader response (e.g., Rosenblatt, 1978) theories, understanding is an

interaction between text content and reader knowledge. What is extremely interesting is how prominent such interactions were in the self-reported processes summarized here. Prior knowledge plays many roles during processing of a text, including a number that readers can consciously report.

As this chapter continues, there are more reports of behaviors that make sense in light of theory and other empirical outcomes. It is impressive just how many different reading behaviors and reactions can occur and how much of this behavior is conscious, at least some of the time. Thus, although it is not surprising that monitoring is prominent in reading, which is taken up in the next section, what is surprising are the many different types of information that readers keep track of.

MONITORING

The think-alouds are informative about the richness of readers' monitoring. Monitoring can stimulate readers to continue processing text in the same way they have done up to this point (i.e., if the reader monitors that comprehension is going well); alternatively, if comprehension is going poorly, awareness of difficulties can stimulate shifts in processing (e.g., Baker, 1989). Often, it is difficult based on think-aloud data to separate monitoring from shifts in processing induced by monitoring and hence, this section does not attempt to do so, with subsections dedicated to detailing the shifts in processing that are tied to monitoring. Of course, that flags the impossibility of separating monitoring processes and those involved in the identification of meaning and learning from text. Still, because the comprehension and learning processes reviewed in this section are correction or fix-it strategies, they are distinct from the meaning identification and learning processes covered in the last section. We begin by outlining the aspects of reading of which readers can be aware.

Monitoring: Perceptions During Reading

Text Characteristics[8]

Perception of:
1. **Whether text content is relevant to the reading goal**
2. **Difficulty of the text**

---

[8]Studies making major contribution to this list: Bazerman (1985), Christopherson et al. (1981), Earthman (1989, 1992), Graves & Frederiksen (1991), Johnston & Afflerbach (1985), Kintgen (1983), Lytle (1982), Shearer et al. (1993), Wood & Zakaluk (1992), Wyatt et al. (1993).

3. Author's style/style of text; structure of the text (e.g., genre, purpose of the text) (e.g., "The *author* reveals the familial relationships slowly to have the *reader* guess and generate hypotheses about them"; Graves & Frederiksen, 1991, p. 12)

4. Linguistic characteristics of text, including lexical/morphological (e.g., "ending of *mope* is odd"; Graves & Frederiksen, 1991, p. 5)/ syntactic/cohesive/topic/punctuation (e.g., "Here the syntax is abridged"; Graves & Frederiksen, 1991, p. 9)/typographical characteristics/type or style of language

5. Specific biases reflected in text content, specific expectations of the text author about the readership

6. Relation of this part of text to larger themes in the text (e.g., "Now, clearly we're in the area of racism with the condescending wife, the white in this case, saying 'Would you like to be my maid?' "; Graves & Frederiksen, 1991, p. 10)

7. Relation of this text to other sources, including whether material in this text is taken from another source

8. When text is ambiguous or potentially so (i.e., awareness of alternative interpretations of text as written) (e.g., "The meaning of 'look down her throat' is not clear"; Graves & Frederiksen, 1991, p. 5; "That's not what the author said before"; Christopherson et al., 1981)

9. Relationship between own background knowledge (or lack of it) and the content of the text
   A. When text contradicts a belief held by the reader (e.g., "Culture here is being used to describe a very different thing than I usually think of 'culture' as an anthropologist"; Johnston & Afflerbach, 1985, p. 222)
   B. Whether information in text was known previously (e.g., "I didn't know that"; Christopherson et al., 1981)
   C. When reader does not possess background knowledge permitting comprehension of what is being read

10. Tone of the text

In summary, there can be awareness of text at a variety of levels, from very broad characteristics such as the difficulty of the text, its style, and its relationship to what one believes or knows already, to very specific characteristics such as the spelling of individual words and the adequacy of particular punctuation marks. Just as there is much about a text that readers can consciously process, there is much about their own processing of text that readers can monitor.

Meaningful Processing of Text[9]

Perception of:

1. **One's purpose in reading the text**
   A. **Information being sought**
   B. **Categories of information relevant to goal**
   C. **Awareness of what is required to complete the reading task at hand**

2. **Own behaviors/strategies in processing text (e.g., aware of when moving forward or backward to resolve questions about meaning; whether and when attentive; when integrating information across different parts of text)**

3. **Reading behaviors/strategies as in the service of the reading goal**

4. **One's typical reactions to the type of text being read**

5. **The difference in reaction to the text compared to typical reactions to this type of reading (e.g., "I'd normally go and look that up")**

6. **Effectiveness of processes and strategies used to determine meaning (e.g., whether moving forward or backward resulted in resolving the question that motivated the forward or backward search of text)**

7. **Cognitive capacity available and when comprehension processes are challenging capacity limit (e.g., awareness of when a great deal of effort is being extended in trying to understand text or when information that needs to be processed is exceeding short-term capacity)**

8. **When there has been progress in determining meaning, although there is more to go (i.e., awareness that some things are not yet understood, with the expectation that gaps in understanding will be filled as reading proceeds)**
   A. **When automatic and without effort**
   B. **When problems in comprehension/ambiguities are being resolved**
   C. **When problems in comprehension/ambiguities are not being resolved**

9. **Whether overall meaning of text is comprehended or reading goal is accomplished**
   A. **When automatic and without effort (e.g., subject simply muttering, "I see," as reading text; Christopherson et al., 1981)**

---

[9]Studies making major contribution to this list: Afflerbach (1990a), Caron (1989), Christopherson et al. (1981), Earthman (1989, 1992), Guthrie et al. (1991), Kintgen (1983), Lytle (1982), Olson et al. (1981), Wood & Zakaluk (1992).

    B. When point just encountered in text resolves previous main problem in comprehension

    C. When an ambiguity in the text is resolved

    D. When text is not understood (e.g., subject utters, "I don't understand"; Christopherson et al., 1981)

10. **Text getting easier to read as meaning becomes more certain**

11. **When the end of a unit of meaning has occurred**

12. **When the reading goal has been achieved (e.g., finding particular piece of information that is sought)**

Most reading goals can only be accomplished by first understanding text, and readers seem very aware of whether they are understanding what they are reading. They are also aware of what they are doing to understand, such as reflected in this self-report: "Sometimes what I do is just what I did right now, is I sort of scan it, and I try to pick up major authors" (Wyatt et al., 1993, p. 59). Readers can be aware of the strategic processes they are using to understand at several levels—what processes are expended, whether the processes are effective, and whether they require great effort to carry out. Thus, one of Johnston and Afflerbach's (1985) readers revealed pessimism about a particular reading process: "Going slow wasn't helping me" (p. 222). Another of Johnston and Afflerbach's (1985) readers expressed awareness of short-term capacity limitations in relating, "I don't know if it's fatigue or what, but some of the stuff . . . the earlier stuff is starting to slip away a bit" (p. 222).

A down side of reading is that sometimes what is read is not understood. There was evidence in the think-alouds of the many different types of difficulties that readers can monitor. Monitoring of various text characteristics and task requirements by readers is critical to regulation of reading processes, with readers consciously aware of how text qualities and reading goals/task demands affect processing decisions. Such complex perception-processing relationships are taken up next.

Problems [10]

Recognizing:

1. **Loss of concentration**

2. **Reading too quickly (e.g., decoding is occurring, but comprehension is low)**

3. **Reading too slowly (e.g., what has been comprehended is decaying)**

---

[10]Studies making major contribution to this list: Graves & Frederiksen (1991), Guthrie et al. (1991), Haas & Flower (1988), Kintgen (1983), Kucan (1993), Lytle (1982), Pritchard (1990a).

4. **Text is poorly written**
   A. Meaning of a word or phrase is unclear (ambiguous)
   B. Discontinuity in text, either within or between sentences (e.g., parts of the text conflict with one another)
5. **Unfamiliar terms in text**
6. **Failure to understand** what has been read or achieve one's reading goal (e.g., the goal of finding a particular piece of information)
   A. Meaning of word, clause, or paragraph remains unknown or unclear despite comprehension efforts (e.g., "I don't know what glibness is, so it is still confusing"; Haas & Flower, 1988, p. 175)
   B. Meaning of word, clause, or paragraph remains unknown or unclear despite comprehension efforts, but reader believes subsequent text is likely to reveal what is going on
7. **Lack of background knowledge** is affecting comprehension negatively
8. **Inconsistency between personal beliefs and information in text**; inconsistency between text meaning and opinions of authoratative sources
9. Inconsistency of one's expectations about meaning and information encountered in the text; conflict between interpretation made previously and new information in text

Problems during reading can be due to text characteristics, reader characteristics, or interactions between text and reader. On the text side, there are a number of ways that text can be poorly written, from problems at the word level to the overall meaning of the passage. On the reader side, difficulties can be due to lack of background for text topic or insufficient lexical knowledge. There can be difficulties due to reader–text interactions; for example, when beliefs of readers clash with opinions expressed in texts.

In the first section of this chapter, dedicated to identification of meaning, much attention was devoted to how meaning construction begins with initial expectations about meaning, which are modified and refined in light of the actual content of the text. Those behaviors are taken up again in this subsection because readers report awareness of such inconsistencies in their think-alouds. Perhaps more optimistically, they also often report that they expect that additional reading will clear up the difficulties, as in this reader comment from Graves and Frederiksen (1991):

> One of the things that's going on here is that the reader has to piece out and follow and see who's who . . . because it's representing a dialogue where . . . the internal context makes the references clear and the reader, who's in the external context . . . can't follow exactly who's who at this point *but obviously . . . figuring out the puzzle will happen . . . as the text goes on. . . .* (p. 20)

Hypothesis activation and revision is taken up again in a subsequent subsection, when the processing stimulated by perceptions of inconsistency are taken up. In short, the hypothesis–hypothesis testing–hypothesis modification cycle (i.e., coming to understand a text) involves complex interactions between prior knowledge, text, processes for identifying meaning, monitoring, and fix-it processes. Because monitoring and fix-it processes can never be separated, they are taken up jointly in later subsections.

Monitoring and the Stimulation of Cognitive Processing: Activation of Processes to Accommodate Text Characteristics/Task Demands[11]

1. Subjects make decisions about how much to interpret text strictly (e.g., literally) or liberally (e.g., going beyond the information in the text by extensively relating to prior knowledge) depending on their goal in reading or the task demand that is on them
2. Decision to rank order reading tasks or goals based on judgment that not all are attainable given contextual constraints (e.g., information load of text, familiarity of text, time available)
3. Decision to skip material—perhaps following deliberation about the potential gains in knowledge from reading it in light of the effort required to do so—because aware that to-be-skipped content is one of the following:
   A. Familiar
   B. Unnecessary details
   C. Text does not contain enough task-/goal-relevant information to make the effort to get the meaning worth it
   D. Difficult enough so that it is unlikely to be understood anyway
4. Decision to skim material, because aware that to-be-skimmed content is one of the following:
   A. Familiar
   B. Unnecessary details
5. Decision to read material carefully, because aware that to-be-read material is one or more of the following:
   A. Unfamiliar
   B. Difficult
   C. Important
   D. Interesting
6. Decision to construct the meaning of text carefully because aware that the text is difficult (e.g., abstract, torturous syntax)

---

[11]Studies making major contribution to this list: Bazerman (1985), Deegan (1993), Earthman (1989, 1992), Kintgen (1983), Shearer et al. (1993), Wyatt et al. (1993).

7. Decision to reset reading goal at a lower level because it is apparent that the reader will not be able to fulfill original reading goal by reading this text (e.g., information in text that might be used to fulfill original goal is too difficult)

8. Decision to look up background material in other sources because aware that other knowledge is required to make sense of what is in a current text

9. Decision to dispense with processing of some part of text because of awareness of potential capacity overload (e.g., material is difficult, extremely unfamiliar, or poorly written and would require great effort to understand)

10. Decision to focus on some content and not other material because of beliefs about processing strengths and weaknesses (e.g., deciding to focus on tables in an article rather than text because reader believes he or she is better at understanding tabled information)

11. Decision to reread material in one section because it is not yet understood

12. Decision to reread material in one section because it is interesting

13. Decision to just keep reading in hope that later content will become clearer

14. Attempt to pinpoint confusions

Readers are aware of many different aspects of text and the reading task they are performing from the outset of reading. Their perceptions of the text and how it relates to their task/reading goals does much to shape the processing of text, with readers processing some parts of text superficially and others very carefully. Thus, one of Wyatt et al.'s (1993) subjects was reading an article in order to write a paper on problem solving, with awareness of this goal shaping reading: "One of the reasons that I'm reading this paper is so that I can write . . . [a] paper, looking at how they're defining problem-solving, which is down here" (Wyatt et al., 1993, p. 59).

A great deal of the control of the processing documented in the first section of this chapter is due to monitoring of text and task characteristics. Good readers not only know what they are doing, but why they are doing it, ever aware of the characteristics of text they are confronting and their own reading goals. For example, Johnston and Afflerbach (1985) reported that readers were aware of when their cognitive capacity was being challenged by the demands of text and acted to reduce those demands, as reflected in the following online comment: "Feeling that this thing better be pieced together before we go on . . . to avoid complete chaos" (p. 222). Johnston and Afflerbach (1985) also observed that sometimes readers recognize that their original reading goal is not being served by reading of this text, perhaps because of their own limitations, and they reset the goal at a lower level, such as in the following example: "Aside from just talking about circadian rhythms, that's about as much as I can gather at this point" (p. 223).

Readers know a lot about themselves as readers and use such awareness to make decisions about how to read. Consider this self-report of awareness and its influence on reading: "I can usually get a lot by looking at tables, and so I typically look at tables" (Wyatt et al., 1993, p. 59).

The role of monitoring in regulating reading has been especially salient to research psychologists when readers detect difficulties in comprehension and react to those difficulties (e.g., Markman, 1977, 1981). Not surprisingly, the think-alouds reflected awareness of comprehenson problems that led to reactions intended to remedy the comprehension problems.

Activation of Processing Due to Awareness of Difficulties at the Word or Phrase Level[12]

1. Evaluating the importance of an unknown word or phrase to the overall meaning of the text before deciding whether to expend effort to determine the unknown word or phrase's meaning

   A. Deciding the unknown word or phrase is not important to understand in order to get the meaning of the text or to meet the reader's goal for reading, and hence skipping the word or phrase (e.g., "Podsnappian" in a text read by one of Johnston & Afflerbach's, 1985, subjects)

   B. Deciding the unknown word or phrase is important to understand in order to get the meaning of the text and hence effort is expended to identify it (using one of the methods considered in this subsection)

2. Greater attention paid to unknown word or phrase (e.g., rereading and/or restating text when an unfamiliar word or phrase is encountered)

   A. Conscious questioning (e.g., "What does *perpetuity* mean?"; see Pritchard, 1990a)

   B. Rereading of text containing unknown word or phrase

   C. Attempted restating of text containing unknown word or phrase

   D. Because the importance of the word, which was originally read over because the reader deemed it unimportant, now becomes clear

3. Use of context clues to interpret a word or phrase

   A. Reading ahead in the text to figure out an unknown word/phrase

---

[12]Studies making major contribution to this list: Deegan (1993), Earthman (1989, 1992), Hare (1981), Johnston & Afflerbach (1985), Kintgen (1983), Olshavsky (1976–1977), Pritchard (1990a).

B. Backtracking in the text to figure out an unknown word

C. Determining the type of word (e.g., syntactically and semantically) that it is likely to be based on context clues

D. Attempting to understand an unfamiliar word or phrase with respect to activated schemata (i.e., if the missing word or phrase can be related to a variable in an activated schema, that variable is used to suggest what the unknown word or phrase might be)

E. Summing up what is known so far in order to figure out the problematic word or phrase

F. Attempting to infer which of several meanings might be appropriate in this context

G. Attempting to substitute a synonym for a difficult word

H. Use structural clues in the word

4. A candidate meaning for unknown word/phrase is generated, with subsequent evaluation of the reasonableness of the sentence containing the word/phrase with that meaning inserted

A. If the meaning does not seem to fit, another attempt to figure out meaning is made (e.g., by relating it to some other schema activated by the text)

B. If an acceptable meaning for an unknown word/phrase is not found given the assumed meaning of the context, the context meaning may be re-evaluated and potentially reinterpreted to fit what the reader thinks the unknown word/phrase might mean

C. If nothing works in producing a meaning that makes sense in the context, the reader gives up and moves on

5. Generating hypotheses about confusing word (or concept)/phrase followed by attempts to determine the adequacy of the hypothesis through additional reading beyond the sentence containing the word/phrase

6. Just keep reading, forgetting about the word

7. Use a dictionary

Encountering an unknown word or phrase does not necessarily result in efforts after meaning. If the reader believes the word or phrase is not essential to determining meaning, he or she can elect to skip the word. If initial attempts to determine the meaning of an unknown word/phrase fail to yield a reasonable candidate meaning, readers sometimes skip the problematic word. Alternatively, if the word or phrase seems important, the reader can consciously attend to the word/phrase more, ponder its meaning in light of context clues, or reflect on its potential meaning by attempting to relate the word/phrase to the currently hypothesized macrostructure. Just as there is evaluation of the hypothesized macrostructure of text as reading proceeds, so it is with respect to the hypothesized meaning of particular words and phrases.

Sometimes words considered at first encounter to be unimportant really are important to understand. Subsequent text can make the importance of a word more obvious, stimulating reconsideration of it, as when one of Johnston and Afflerbach's (1985) participants recognized that *idée fixe* was critical sometime after its first encounter: "Idee fixe . . . I've never heard of that before and I'm wondering if I read it right . . . [re-reads sentence] . . . I couldn't put that together at all . . . I'm going to go back . . . [re-reads sentence] . . . I'm stopping here and still trying to put this sentence together . . . the same word threw me [idée fixe]" (p. 217).

Of course, not understanding the meaning of a word or phrase is not particularly consequential compared to not understanding the text as a whole, which occurs often and is monitored. Again, readers react in a variety of ways when there is failure to understand large messages in text—a subject that is taken up next.

Activation of Processing Due to Awareness of Difficulties in Understanding Meaning Beyond the Word or Phrase Level[13]

1. Although aware of the comprehension difficulty (i.e., ambiguity, incompleteness of presentation up until this point in the text), doing nothing:
   A. If the reader feels this part of text is not important to understand
   B. If reader feels ambiguity/lack of clarity is due to his or her own effort or ability (e.g., "I am not smart enough to understand this")
   C. If reader feels ambiguity/lack of clarity is due to author failure (i.e., "This author writes poorly")
2. Once aware of a comprehension difficulty, doing one of the following:
   A. Stating the failure to understand
   B. Reading slowly and carefully
   C. Suspending judgment about what the meaning is (i.e., simply continuing to read in hope of a later resolution)
   D. Pausing from reading to scan the text to find the source of difficulty
   E. Carefully analyzing information presented in text thus far
      a. Restating text when unsure of meaning of sentence, paragraph
      b. Summarizing meaning of text up to this point when in doubt about meaning

---

[13]Studies making major contribution to this list: Bereiter & Bird (1985), Deegan (1993), Earthman (1989, 1992), Hare (1981), Kintgen (1983), Lytle (1982), Olshavsky (1976–1977), Shearer et al. (1993), Wyatt et al. (1993).

    c. If contradictions seem to be between paragraphs, analyze sentence by sentence; if contradictions seem to be between sentences within a paragraph, word-by-word analysis of relevant sentences

F. Rereading last section read (i.e., when failing to see connection between overall hypothesized meaning and meaning of last paragraph)

    a. From the beginning of a problematic section of text, taking problem-solving stance to figure out the meaning (e.g., analyzing torturous syntax): Try to get rid of problem through constructing an inference, closer examination of text, or rejecting information in the text

    b. Rereading parts of text that were understood in order to figure out how to connect the most recent section to what went before

G. Formulating a question that captures the perplexity, with these questions making clear what information to look for in subsequent text (i.e., setting "watchers" for particular information; e.g., "Is Miss Emily Black?" or "Do you ever find out what might happen to Homer?"; Bereiter & Bird, 1985)

H. Looking ahead to see if there is information later in text that might resolve the comprehension difficulty (e.g., with "watchers" playing a role in this if reader has some idea about what type of information might be helpful; Bereiter & Bird; 1985)

I. Re-attending to parts of the text most likely to be understood reliably because reader's prior knowledge is well developed with respect to information in these sections

3. Once several potential interpretations of text are recognized, ones not obviously consistent with one another, reader responds in one of the following ways

A. Carefully analyzing text to decide between these alternatives, and subsequently rejecting some of them

    a. Perhaps changing some assumptions about the meaning of the text up until this point (i.e., modifying the hypothesized macrostructure)

B. Constructing inferences to account for the perceived discrepancies in meaning in the text (i.e., recognizing seeming contradictions in text and contradictory interpretations, stimulating generation of integrative structures to accomodate them; e.g., rationalizing that different points of view are being presented in the text because this is an introduction, which should represent the diverse perspectives on a problem)

C. Recognizing that the theme that is currently confusing cannot be reconciled with other interpretations made thus far and thus, bringing in new information based on prior knowledge in an attempt to resolve difficulty in understanding

D. Attempting to formulate a new macroproduction about what this text is about, one consistent with all the information presented in the text thus far as understood by the reader

4. If a part of text cannot be understood completely, shifting focus to other parts of the text or questions that have not been considered but also need to be resolved.

5. If a text cannot be understood, attempting to think of an analogy that would make the meaning clearer

6. If a reading-related goal is determined unattainable, adjusting the goal

7. Looking up some of the references cited in the write-up (i.e., source documents)—or at least looking to the reference list to find out what work informed the current writing—or seeking other information from other sources

8. Reading on without figuring out an interpretation when a convincing interpretation cannot be discerned from the text by the reader (i.e., giving up on finding an interpretation of the point in question and moving on)

9. Distorting some of the information in the text in order to construct an interpretation that is consistent with a tentative hypothesis

10. Distraction
    A. Thinking about things other than reading
    B. Falling asleep either mentally or actually

11. Simply giving up on understanding the text and quitting

Good readers are effective planners, with those plans informed by their personal reading goals, which in turn affect their monitoring as they read (i.e., how they set their "watchers," to use Bereiter & Bird's, 1985, term). Thus, the following comment reflects awareness of goals in deciding what to look for in a text: "So what I'm going to do is I'm gonna start looking at the background and theory because I want to see what kind of a . . . , where this person comes from his theoretical perspective" (Wyatt et al., 1993, p. 61).

Potential difficulties in understanding are often flagged by contradictions between what the reader believes the text means and new information in the text inconsistent with the hypothesized overall meaning. Such contradictions produce a number of reactions, from simply continuing to read, confident that it will all become clear later, to abandoning the current overall interpretation in pursuit of one that would be consistent with all of the information encountered in the text thus far. These reactions depend on both reader and text factors. For example, how one reacts depends on whether the reader believes he or she might be able to resolve the contradiction based on general competence as a reader or prior knowledge related to the topic of this reading. Whether a reader really can generate inferences that reconcile seeming contradictions depends greatly on prior knowledge. Text factors play a role in that if the reader perceives that the problem is simply poor writing, there is little incentive for the reader to attempt to figure out the meaning of the text. In addition, given the across-text comparisons and analyses that need to be carried out to resolve many comprehension difficulties, it would be expected that better organized text would be easier to reanalyze.

Monitoring does not occur only as reading proceeds, but continues after reading is completed, regulating processing of text that occurs after the initial reading. Readers monitor whether they comprehended what they have just completed processing. As is the case during reading, there are diverse reactions to feelings that comprehension/memory are not as complete as they could be.

Post-Reading Monitoring and Decisions to Process Additionally[14]

1. If reader is aware that the hypothesized macrostructure active at the end of a reading is consistent with all of the information in text, and important questions that came up during the reading have been answered, he or she is not likely to search text for additional information in order to understand text

2. If reader senses inconsistency between hypothesized macrostructure active at the end of a reading and some of the information in the text, or important questions that came up during reading have not been answered, reader continues search for meaning
   A. Material may be skimmed to "put it together"
   B. Material in text may be systematically reviewed to firm up meaning, short of rereading
   C. Listing the information overtly
   D. Material can be reread, either in part or whole
   E. Rereading may occur after some period of time has passed in order for the material to incubate

---

[14]Studies making major contribution to this list: Johnston & Afflerbach (1985), Kintgen (1983).

Summary

Monitoring occurs throughout the reading cycle for the skilled reader, simultaneously occurring at a number of levels. Although all such awareness does not inevitably lead to cognitive action—indeed, sensing that a text has been understood can result in inaction—there are many occasions when readers react to feelings of low comprehension with new efforts at determining meaning. Awareness of text and its characteristics also has another effect: It can lead to evaluations about the text, its structure, and content (see especially Wyatt et al., 1993). This issue is taken up in the next section.

EVALUATING

Readers self-report many evaluations as they are reading. Often these occur in reaction to particular bits of information in text. Other times they are reactions to the text as a whole. Still other times, the readers' disposition is more a determinant of evaluations than the text per se, with a general evaluative stance apparent from the beginning of reading. We consider such consistent reactions before we consider more specific evaluations.

Consistent Evaluative Mindsets[15]

1. **Anticipatory evaluation/affect,** based on their feelings about/prior knowledge of the topic
2. **Acceptance**
    A. **Uncritical acceptance reported when material is from content domain in which reader has no background knowledge**
    B. **Uncritical acceptance when reader assumes that reading is a factual document (i.e., a simple recording of unambiguous facts)**
    C. **Critical acceptance when a reader has considerable knowledge about the text topic and author intention, and reader agrees with the author (or text)**
3. **Skepticism, with wariness heightened to the extent that the material is likely to impact conclusions (knowledge possessed by the reader) considered important by the reader**

---

[15]Studies making major contribution to this list: Afflerbach (1990b), Bazerman (1985), Beach (1972), Charney (1993), Kintgen (1983), Shearer et al. (1993), Squire (1964), Wood & Zakaluk (1992), Wyatt et al. (1993)

4. Reader acutely aware document was written by a particular person with particular biases, purposes, and background knowledge; hence, reader's stance is that the document must be evaluated by determining meanings that are not stated explicitly

Sometimes readers recognize from the very start that they are likely to be evaluative with respect to a text, and likely to react to it affectively. For example, one of Afflerbach's (1990b) subjects related after reading the title, "War of the Ghosts," "I'm thinking I'm probably not going to enjoy this article as well . . . it's not familiar . . . nothing I'm keen on . . . it's fiction . . . and it's not my own interest" (p. 145)." Another student reacted to the same title differently: "This will be a fun thing to read" (p. 145).

Although some readers evidence great consistency in their evaluative stances as they read some texts, evaluations are often much more discriminated. Regardless of whether a reader is globally positive, globally negative, or a mixture of both, evaluations occur with respect to the style and content of text.

Focused Evaluations[16]

Style of the Text

1. Is writing good or bad?
   A. Sophisticated, appropriate vocabulary?
   B. Well-constructed sentences? Syntax? (e.g., "There is a deliberate manipulation of the syntax"; "The lack of punctuation makes this difficult for the reader"; Graves & Frederiksen, 1991, p. 5)
   C. Particularly appealing or unappealing phrasing?
   D. Relation of quality of writing to quality of arguments
      a. Is good writing dressing up poor arguments or are good arguments being harmed by poor writing?
      b. Does bad writing reflect a poorly framed problem, inadequately defined assumptions, weak methods, unclear results, or poor understanding?
   E. Is overall structure effective . . . (e.g., in conveying author's purpose)?
2. Are examples effective, compelling?
3. Physical text (e.g., "This is a bad copy!")

---

[16]Studies making major contribution to this list: Bazerman (1985), Beach (1972), Caron (1989), Charney (1993), Christopherson et al. (1981), Deegan (1993), Earthman (1989, 1992), Graves & Frederiksen (1991), Haas & Flower (1988), Kintgen (1983), Kucan (1993), Lundeberg (1987), Lytle (1982), Pritchard (1990a), Schwegler & Shamoon (1991), Shearer et al. (1993), Squire (1964), Trabasso & Suh (1993), Wood & Zakaluk (1992), Wyatt et al. (1993).

Content of the Text

1. Deciding early in the reading based on salient information (e.g., author, title, abstract) whether piece contains important information and deserves to be processed carefully (or at all)
   A. Will piece enrich reader knowledge? (e.g., is it important to know?)
   B. Is reading relevant to current work/goals/project?
   C. Is there information in this text not encountered in previous reading?
2. Approval/disapproval of the content, arguments made, and so on
   A. Message in the text (e.g., "I don't think this would work for the man in the street"; Haas & Flower, 1988, p. 176)
   B. Development of concepts, arguments, quality of evidence
      a. Are arguments complete? That is, unambiguous, exhaustive, covering all sides of an issue?
      b. Are the arguments/conclusions intellectually sophisticated?
      c. Are the arguments valid? Based on logically compelling evidence as developed in writing? (e.g., Bazerman, 1985)
   C. Quality (sophistication) of content relative to the perceived sophistication of the writer (i.e., different standard for student vs. senior scholar)
   D. Does it meet the standards of the discipline/profession?
   E. Content relative to perceived goal/purpose of the author (i.e., did author accomplish his or her purpose? Does the writing do what it promises to do from the outset?)
   F. Content relative to the audience author is addressing (i.e., is the content at a level appropriate to the audience addressed?)
   G. Is content current or novel?
   H. Is there an attempt to interpret at all or to go beyond the superficial? Does author offer a new slant on the problem under consideration?
   I. Is content trustworthy?
      a. Plausible based on what reader already knows?
      b. Plausible based on reader beliefs?
      c. Ideas consistent with positions held by authorities on the topic of the text?
   J. Is content interesting?
   K. Are interpretations consistent with facts of text? Are interpretations reasonable or novel?

    L. Evaluating positiveness/negativeness of states of affairs described/implied by text

    M. Evaluating characters or characteristics of characters covered in the writing

3. Topic/comment strategy: Making evaluative comment for each topic, or comments for at least some topics, covered in a text

4. Revising evaluations as text is processed further

5. Overt affective reactions

    A. Positive reactions, including satisfaction, such as concluding that what was learned was worth the effort

    B. Surprise

    C. Laughter

    D. Puzzlement

    E. Negative reactions

      a. Boredom

      b. Frustration

      c. Swearing

      d. Other (giving the raspberry)

    F. Anxiety (e.g., fearing failure to comprehend, believing it may not be possible for him or her to "get the meaning")

6. Approval/disapproval of characters, places, circumstances in a story or article

7. Long-delayed evaluation following postreading reflection, reading of other work, or some other activity (researching to better understand the significance of a text)

We encountered many examples in the think-aloud studies of readers offering evaluations of what they read. Here is a sample from Haas and Flower (1988) where the authors told of Bob's reaction to some psychology text: "Well, I don't think they're too simple for a complex world. I don't think these are very simple things being said here. I think the situations—women, children, and men—I think they're pretty complex . . . so I don't understand why it said 'too simple for the complex world' " (p. 173). Rogers (1991) offered an example of a reader making an evaluation of a text character: "I wouldn't want him as my father . . ." (p. 413). The influence of prior knowledge on evaluations came through in this report by a reader in Wyatt et al.'s (1993) study:

And so, you know, I'm sitting here now thinking this paper does everything that I think it shouldn't do. For instance, it really doesn't measure in any kind of detail the students' conceptual understandings. . . . Not only that, so this thing does not measure the impact of conceptual knowledge, but then they sort of ignored treatment. And the treatment that they do is fairly terrible. (p. 62)

The interaction between prior knowledge and text content also was obvious when the same subject remarked, "And it sort of gets me angry that we don't use better instruments" (Wyatt et al., 1993, p. 63).

Sometimes evaluations are long delayed, with the reader recognizing the significance of a piece of work only long after the original reading, as when one of Bazerman's (1985) physicists reported, "Sometimes I miss things . . . I think things are not particularly interesting, and then I kick myself later for having missed it" (p. 249).

In short, evaluations occur at a number of levels when skilled readers read. Sometimes they occur on-line and sometimes after a reading is concluded. That relatively few of the self-report studies included evaluative remarks may tell us that analyses in many think-aloud studies were not sensitive to evaluative processing. Our supposition is that much of evaluation was folded into monitoring in some studies, a supposition substantiated by a very high correlation (i.e., .77) between monitoring processes and evaluation in Wyatt et al. (1993). One argument against this correlation is that it substantiates that monitoring and evaluation should be considered as one process. We resist that temptation, however, for the reactions we classified as monitoring seem much more dispassionate than the reactions we classified as evaluation. Monitoring is focused on making processing decisions and is future oriented—what to do next; evaluation focuses on the worth of what has been processed.

SUMMARY

The conscious processing that goes on during skilled reading can be enormously complex, as substantiated by the length of this chapter summarizing self-reported thinking during reading. Still, there is a striking orderliness to the processing that occurs. That is, it is possible to summarize all the thinking that goes on into a number of categories that are familiar to cognitive psychologists and reading response researchers. Thus, skilled readers know and use many different procedures (strategies) in coming to terms with text: They proceed generally from front to back of documents when reading. Good readers are selectively attentive. They sometimes make notes. They predict, paraphrase, and back up when confused. They try to make inferences to fill in the gaps in text and in their understanding of what they have read. Good readers intentionally attempt to integrate across the text. They do not settle for literal meanings but rather interpret what they have read, sometimes constructing images, other times identifying categories of information in text, and on still other occasions engaging in arguments with themselves about what a reading might mean. After making their way through text, they have a variety of ways of firming up their understanding and memory of the messages in the text, from explicitly attempting to summarize to self-questioning about the text to rereading and reflecting. The many procedures used by skilled readers are appropriately and opportunistically coordinated, with the reader using the processes needed to meet current reading goals, confronting the demands of reading at the moment, and preparing for demands that are likely in the future (e.g., the need to recall text content for a test).

Such finely articulated use of comprehension processes requires massive knowledge of when and where various procedures apply—that is, massive *metacognition*. For the most part, long-term metacognitive knowledge must be inferred from think-alouds, although there were certainly occasions in the self-reports when readers stated their awareness of processing options in particular situations and the contextual characteristics that would call for particular types of process. For example, recall Wade et al.'s (1990) reader who knew that the way to review text before a test was to read the underlinings and marginal notes constructed during reading.

The finely articulated use of comprehension processes also requires the generation of metacognitive information as reading proceeds—it requires consistent awareness of the task demands and progress made in meeting those demands. *Monitoring* produces such metacognitive awareness. Although reading researchers (see Baker, 1989) have known for a very long time that many aspects of text processing are monitored, there is no analysis in the literature that provides a window on the full complexity of monitoring as well as the analysis offered in this chapter. There is monitoring of minute details (e.g., awareness that words are misspelled) and monitoring of whether a text is being understood as a whole. There is monitoring that focuses on text features (e.g., linguistic and syntactic characteristics), readers' processing (e.g., demands on short-term capacity), and interactions between text and reader characteristics (e.g., awareness of the relationship of one's own prior knowledge to information presented in text). How monitoring affects the use of cognitive procedures was evident in many of the self-reports, with decisions to read carefully, skim, reread, and seek information outside the text following directly from awareness of current processing as well as task and text demands.

In short, cognitive procedures and their regulation through metacognitive mechanisms was apparent in the self-reports. So were other features of reading that are very sensible from the perspective of information processing theory.

The construct of *goals* is salient in information processing conceptions of thinking, from historically important and abstract theories (e.g., Miller et al., 1960), to historically important and applied theories (e.g., Polya, 1954a, 1954b), to modern theoretical (e.g., Schank & Abelson, 1977) and pragmatic (e.g., Deshler & Schumaker, 1988) approaches. Consistent with these analyses, goals were prominent in the processing observed in the self-reports summarized in this chapter. Readers begin reading by constructing a goal for the current text. Whether they quit the text or expend the energy to process it carefully depends on readers' perceptions of the relevance of the text to their current goals. Selectivity in reading is goal driven (e.g., looking for content consistent with the current reading goal), as are all effortful processes intended to increase comprehension and/or memory of text (e.g., taking notes on goal-relevant material). That is, readers are constantly monitoring whether the text being read is relevant to goals. Evaluations of the text as worthwhile or useless can be made only by considering the text in relation to goals.

Central to contemporary information processing analyses of reading (e.g., R. C. Anderson & Pearson, 1984) is nonprocedural knowledge—the many pieces of declarative knowledge one has about the world (see J. R. Anderson, 1983). The effects of *prior knowledge* on processing were salient in the think-alouds reviewed here. Readers can activate knowledge related to the topic of a text even before they begin to read it. Predictions and initial hypotheses about meaning are possible because of such knowledge. Throughout reading, information encountered in text is related to knowledge of the world, with inferences and interpretations possible only because of prior knowledge. Some reading strategies are only possible when a reader possesses prior knowledge, such as attempts to construct analogies to understand text that is initially perceived as vague. Readers monitor whether what is being read is consistent with prior knowledge, sometimes electing to focus on the "news," which expands previous understandings and sometimes rejecting the information in a text because it is just too different from deeply held beliefs and long-standing perspectives. Sensible evaluative conclusions can only be made by readers who possess knowledge permitting a standard against which the current text can be compared.

There was massive support for constructivist theories of knowledge in these self-reports. No one could read the protocols and not appreciate the extensive intellectual activity involved in constructing meaning from text. Determining meaning is a problem-solving, hypothesis-testing activity. Such knowledge construction occurs at many levels, from attempting to get the gist of the text to efforts at understanding individual words. Meaning emerges because of activity enabled by prior knowledge, knowledge that when combined with new messages in text permits construction of new understandings, both of big ideas and small ideas (i.e., definitions of individual words). Indeed, our view of this chapter is that it provides a fine-grained analysis of the nature of constructivist thinking during skilled reading, with construction beginning with a goal or set of goals and continuing as text is overviewed, read the first time, reread, reflected on, and evaluated. As we state this conclusion in linear terms, we emphasize, however, that skilled reading is massively recursive and flexible: Overview, reflection, and evaluation occur and co-occur throughout the reading process, with the order of processing of text impossible to predict, even though it is certain based on the analyses summarized here that text, reader, and contextual characteristics are all involved in the determination of meaning during any single second, minute, or hour of reading. Although the specific processes of the moment are unpredictable, they are clearly orderly, with reader rationality, planfulness, and intentions obvious in every self-report we encountered in the literature. The elegant coordinations that constitute skilled reading become even more obvious in the concluding chapter of this volume, which relates the processing evident in the self-reports to specific contemporary conceptions of reading.

One especially disappointing characteristic of the protocol analysis literature is that the social contextual variables were largely ignored in these studies. Even so, the social aspects of reading were present in some of the reports of subjects determining meaning, monitoring, and evaluating, consistent with our perspective that reading is a socially embedded activity. Reading is wedded to social contexts and social uses: A reader may use knowledge gained from reading to engage in a debate or to share with a colleague. A reader working through a difficult task may monitor the construction of meaning with respect to a social criterion, such as whether enough has been learned from the text to use the information in an upcoming discussion. Readers attempting to determine an author's intent, bias, or agenda often consider the social context in which the text was constructed. When readers engage in dialog with the imagined author, as some of Wyatt et al.'s (1993) participants did, they introduce a social approach to reading, one that forces attention to the writer's purpose and social circumstances.

In closing this chapter, we reiterate the message at the end of the last chapter. This probably will not be the last word on what skilled readers can do when they read. If it were, we would have expected that no new types of processing would have been discerned in studies that we read near the end of the categorization exercise summarized in this chapter. That was not the case, with even the most recently published analyses providing new insights about the thoughts of readers as they read. More positively, from the perspective of the analysis reported here, the new categories emerging in the more recent reports were more on the order of fine tuning, rather than ones suggesting a need to completely overhaul the basic classification scheme. The fact that relatively few adjustments were made for the last few studies integrated into the analysis permits confidence in the classification structure summarized in this chapter. Still, the model is not saturated, and there is always the possibility that someone else might organize the many processes observed in these studies into an alternative theoretical structure other than one based on strategies, monitoring, and evaluation.

Whether this is attempted or not, the think-aloud data available to date and the analysis reported here have implications for a variety of text processing models currently proposed by theorists and researchers. We turn next to theories that are informed by the work reviewed in this book and the framework reported in this chapter.

4

▼▼▼▼▼▼▼

Text Processing in Light of Think-Aloud Analyses of Reading: Constructively Responsive Reading

Explaining how people process text has been an important goal of cognitive psychologists, literary theorists, and others. A variety of models have been proposed. In the first part of this chapter we review some of the more popular models and theories in light of the summary of results from protocol analyses that was presented in chapter 3. On the one hand, the protocol analyses do support the various models of comprehension that have been proposed. That is, the processes specified by each of these models are represented in the think-aloud reports. We expected a degree of congruence between models of text processing and the aggregate findings of think-aloud studies, for think-aloud studies have often been informed and motivated by these models. On the other hand, the verbal report data summarized in chapter 3 does more than provide partial verification of theoretical models. In fact, the verbal report data extend these models, leading to a complex description of reading than specified by any of the previously existing models.

Thus, the second part of this chapter is a model that emanates from our chapter 3 summary of the conscious processes involved in reading. We characterize such reading as "constructively responsive," making the case that excellent readers are actively constructive as they interact with and respond to information in text while reading for a particular purpose.

The third part of this chapter considers the model of constructively responsive reading as a specific example of expertise. In particular, this analysis permits some speculation about the origins of mature constructively responsive reading and the potential implications of the analysis offered here for reading education. The claim is made that constructively responsive reading represents many years of readers' varied experiences and practice in constructing meaning from demanding texts. We develop the case that some reading instructional innovations since the 1980s logically, if anything, should stimulate the development of constructive responsivity during reading, although not nearly enough research has been conducted on the effects (especially long-term effects) of these instructional innovations to know for certain their full impact. First, however, before taking up the theory of constructive responsivity and how it relates to expert theory and contemporary reading instruction, we review the extant theories of text processing and compare them with the model of constructive responsivity we developed from protocol analyses.

PREVIOUS THEORIES OF TEXT PROCESSING

Think-aloud studies have been generated by researchers with different interests and backgrounds, from literary criticism theorists to cognitive psychologists to reading educators. It should not be surprising that the different theories fueling this research emphasize different aspects of text processing. Developed from different theoretical perspectives, the theories provide rich descriptions of different aspects of reading.

Reader Response Theory

Reader response theory was offered as a reaction to the model of literature education that predominated early in the 20th century. In contrast to the perspective that texts have objective meanings, Rosenblatt (1938) proposed that the meanings of texts will vary somewhat from reader to reader. This followed from the observation that people vary in their interpretations of the same text (e.g., Richards, 1929). According to reader response theory, interpretive variability occurs because the meaning of a text involves a transaction between a reader, who has particular perspectives and prior knowledge, and a text, which can affect different readers in different ways (e.g., Beach & Hynds, 1991; Rosenblatt, 1978). What is critical from the perspective of reader response theory is how the reader experiences and reacts to the text.

Sometimes readers respond emotionally to text, often they form impressions of characters in stories, and frequently they relate their personal and cultural experiences to events encountered in text. They may respond to difficult-to-understand text by treating the process of establishing meaning as an exercise in problem solving, requiring probing analysis of text and posing of numerous questions as part of attempting to determine what a text might mean. As part of responding to text, readers sometimes explain events in a text to themselves. Sometimes they judge text, with differences between readers in the criteria used in evaluating text meanings and qualities.

How a reader responds to text depends in part on the reader's interest in the topic of the reading, as well as reader personality characteristics and attitudes (e.g., toward the ideas expressed in the text). Readers who are more cognitively mature sometimes respond differently than less cognitively advanced readers. Background knowledge matters a great deal. For example, a physicist reading a journal article on quantum physics may ably and critically evaluate the text, whereas a reader lacking background knowledge in physics struggles to construct a bare-bones, literal account. Reader knowledge of the content domain of a text can affect responses to it. So can other types of knowledge, such as knowledge of the literary genre, sociocultural knowledge about the appropriateness of various types of responses in different situations, and gender-determined knowledge and attitudes.

Even so, an important point of reader response theory is that the meaning of a text is not completely subjective—there are better and worse interpretations, with better interpretations accounting for more of the elements in a text (Eco, 1990; Rosenblatt, 1938). Still, any reader's experience with a text will be unique because of the reader's personal history, their mood at the moment, and the state of the reader's world at the time the text is encountered.

Rosenblatt (1938, 1978) suggested that literature can permit cognitive experiences that would not or could not occur to the reader otherwise (e.g., a 1990s child in the Canadian maritimes experiencing the thoughts of a 1930s schoolboy growing up on the prairies of Saskatchewan). Literature permits readers to experience different points of view, the social perspectives of different places, peoples, and times. Rosenblatt also contended that by reflecting on one's responses to literature portraying foreign events and alternative points of view, it is possible to learn much about oneself.

Is reader response theory supported by the think-aloud analyses? Consistent with the theory, interpretations and evaluations of text have been reported prominently in protocol analyses of reading. No one could read the various interpretations and evaluations reported in the think-aloud studies without being impressed by their variety. Even when the same text was read by all readers in a study, there were a number of different interpretations and evaluations of it (despite the fact that verbal report data are often selected with an eye to common processes that are shared across subjects.) Moreover, at least some of the readers in these studies have been transported to different times and ways of thinking, as when Lundeberg's (1987) lawyers attempted to gauge the thinking of a supreme court justice who lived long ago. Similarly, Wyatt et al.'s (1993) readers used their experiences as writers and readers as they tried to figure out what the authors of various pieces must have been thinking and attempting to communicate when they were writing the article being read. There definitely is evidence of reading liberating readers from the present in the think-aloud protocols. Readers sometimes experience the perspectives of others through reading; reading can stimulate engagement and contemplation of previously unfamiliar ideas.

Emotional responses to text are common as well in the protocols, consistent with the reader response theoretical perspective that reading is an intense experience, with readers living through their reading, not merely responding cerebrally to words on a page. To the extent that think-aloud studies have examined reactions to text as a function of reader background knowledge, differences due to background have been found (e.g., between experienced historians and undergraduates reading history in Wineberg, 1991), again consistent with reader response theory. Even attempts to learn the information in a text by rote (e.g., strategic repetitions of it, notetaking) are consistent with reader response theory, in that such strategies are expected when the goal of reading a text is to remember its content. (Rosenblatt, 1978, referred to reading for learning as efferent reading, in contrast to aesthetic reading, which is for appreciation of the literature.) Reader response theory predicts readers will attend to a text at various levels of analysis, from the word level to the level of overarching meaning. Reader response theory also predicts readers will attend to their own processes as readers. Of course, as summarized in chapter 3, readers frequently report such awarenesses as they read, monitoring word level processes, overall comprehension, and ongoing processing of text.

Even so, protocol analyses reveal many aspects of text processing that are not specifically addressed by reader response theories. Readers do not just respond to texts, but also anticipate meanings in text (i.e., they make predictions, rather than only react to content once presented). Rather than simply responding to text, sometimes readers are extremely planful in attempting to derive meaning, beginning with overviewing activities, making predictions, formulating plans for evaluating their predictions and getting the most out of the text, and continuing to search for meaning if they monitor that the text has not been understood. Such planfulness is neither the focus of reader response theory nor explained well by it. Try as we might, it is difficult to determine from the think-aloud data reviewed in chapter 3 that the readers in the think-aloud studies were learning much about themselves as they read, which Rosenblatt considered to be an important effect of interpretively responding to texts. This may be due in part to the fact that many researchers purposely steer subjects clear of reflection while reading, believing reflection may move the verbal report into the realm of introspection and away from reporting of processes and strategies.

Reader response theory, with its emphasis on reader prerogative for interpretation, evaluation, and criticism (Rosenblatt, 1978) is more complete than other conceptions of text processing, ones offered by cognitive psychologists, ones that are discussed later in this section. In covering readers' coding of objective text, interpretations, and evaluations, reader response theory touches on the broad categories of human constructive reactions to texts, emphasizing the critical role of reader knowledge in meaning construction processes. In doing so, reader response theory is not very specific, however, leaving many of the particular coding, interpretive, and evaluative processes covered in chapter 3 not elucidated.

Although reader awareness of words, overall meaning, and reactions are specified as critical in reader response theory, there is little explication as to exactly how such awareness is manifested, and reader response theory is silent to many of the monitoring processes specified in chapter 3. The cognitive theories that follow in this chapter are much more specific with respect to the processes they include in their conceptions of reading, although none of the positions covered in this section include the great range of response categories included in reader response theory. Somewhat ironically, the oldest of the text processing models reviewed here—Rosenblatt's (1938) *Literature as Exploration*, the first explication of reader response theory—is perhaps the most adequate of the text processing frameworks in its scope, even if it is vague in its specifics. The second part of this chapter offers a theory, based on the think-aloud analyses, that combines the scope of reader response theory with the specifics of modern cognitive theories. We call this theory constructive responsivity, and we acknowledge beforehand that the models reviewed in this chapter have had varying degrees of influence on our thoughts related to constructive responsivity.

Baker and Brown's (1984) Metacognitive Theory

Baker and Brown (1984) offered one of the more complete models of text processing emanating from cognitive psychology and argued forcefully that being metacognitive is essential for skilled reading. Their work in particular highlighted the metacognitive process of comprehension monitoring as critical to self-regulation: Comprehension monitoring is the active awareness of whether one is understanding or remembering text being processed. Such monitoring was viewed by Baker and Brown as essential to planful use of strategies and shifts in strategies during reading, such as when readers change tactics once they are aware that their current approach is not permitting comprehension. Baker and Brown's view is that mature reading involves active evaluation of understanding as reading occurs, with corrective actions initiated (e.g., rereading, slower reading) when miscomprehension is sensed. Less mature readers are less strategic largely because they fail to monitor the state of their comprehension as they read.

Baker and Brown (1984) were selective in examining the strategies that contribute to skilled reading. They focused on reading for main ideas, making use of text structures in abstracting meaning from text, self-interrogating, and summarizing (especially as a test of whether text is understood or can be remembered). Their work was influenced by an important training study on middle-grade students by Palincsar and Brown (1984), in which weak readers were taught to predict, question, clarify, and summarize as they read.

Baker and Brown (1984) highlighted that it was essential for readers to know when and where to use the strategies they knew. Knowing strategies was one thing, but knowing when to use them appropriately was very different. Using strategies appropriately depended on two types of metacognition—knowledge of the situational appropriateness of particular comprehension processes as well as knowledge of ongoing comprehension as permitted by monitoring processes.

Baker (1989) updated and expanded on the 1984 perspective. In doing so, Baker cited prominently a number of think-aloud reports, as had Baker and Brown (1984). More strategies were cited, many of which were identified through think-aloud research. Comprehension monitoring was discussed more analytically, with seven different monitoring standards specified (i.e., monitoring understanding of individual words, syntactic and grammatic correctness, consistency of the text with external reality, propositional cohesiveness, cohesiveness of the overall text structure, and informational completeness; see also Baker, 1985). Consistent with the outcomes of a rather large number of studies conducted in the mid 1980s (e.g., Glenberg & Epstein, 1987; see Pressley & Ghatala, 1990), Baker (1989) was less sanguine about adult monitoring of text processing than Baker and Brown (1984) had been: That is, there were many reports of monitoring failures by adults in the mid 1980s, with Baker (1989) reflecting awareness of the metacognitive deficiencies of many adult readers, at least in some text processing situations. Even so, skilled reading was still portrayed by Baker (1989) as strategic and monitored: "[adults] . . . who are better readers, and who are more successful students seem to have greater awareness and control of their own cognitive activities while reading" (p. 33).

The Baker and Brown (1984) perspective fares well in light of our analysis of the think-aloud protocols. Conscious processing during reading involves many strategies, including all of those cited in Baker and Brown's (1984) chapter and Baker's (1985, 1989) later writing (i.e., they all appear in the chapter 3 summary). The complexity of monitoring that Baker (1985, 1989) related is mirrored in the think-aloud data as well. Readers do monitor characteristics of the text and the state of their own processing, and consistent with Baker and Brown (1984), report that they sometimes alter their processing in light of such monitoring.

Much of the research summarized in chapter 3 complements and extends the Baker and Brown (1984) model. Even so, there is much summarized in chapter 3 that is not reflected in the Baker and Brown (1984) model, or at least, it is not covered very completely. For example, although Baker and Brown comment on orientation to main ideas as a strategy, their analysis is silent on the many processes contributing to the identification and learning of the main ideas of a passage. The think-aloud analyses reveal a variety of overviewing, initial reading, and postreading processes that are part of understanding the central ideas of a text, processes not represented in Baker and Brown (1984). Also, inferential processes receive little mention in Baker and Brown, although the think-alouds make clear that there are many types of inferences made consciously by skilled readers. The same is true for integrative and interpretive activities, both of which can be thought of broadly as sets of inferential processes. Although some aspects of monitoring cited by Baker (1985, 1989) involve evaluation (e.g., monitoring the semantic completeness or structural integrity of text), evaluation is not nearly *what is domain language?*

as salient in Baker's writing as it is in the think-alouds summarized in chapter 3. Although domain knowledge is not prominently featured in the Baker and Brown (1984) model, verbal report data again extend and enrich our understanding of the value and uses of domain knowledge. Specifically, verbal reports describe the strong influence of readers' domain knowledge on understanding information in the text.

According to Baker and Brown (1984), reading can be understood in terms of the exact information processes of the reader, which they operationalize as strategies and monitoring for the most part. Readers who carry out strategies efficiently comprehend and remember the objective information in texts according to this perspective. In 1984 this model represented a reasonable summary of some of the most influential findings produced by cognitive psychologists interested in text processes. Since then, there have been enormous gains in our understanding of inferential processes in comprehension (e.g., Graesser, 1993a, 1993b) and the centrality of interpretive reactions (e.g., Beach & Hynds, 1991) as part of understanding the messages in text. Also, subsequent work demonstrated that skillful reading involves complex articulations between strategies and knowledge, and not one or the other (e.g., see Pressley, 1994; Pressley, Borkowski, & Schneider, 1987, 1989). To be certain, however, Baker and Brown (1984) were not the only scientists in the mid 1980s to push either strategies or knowledge.

R. C. Anderson and Pearson's (1984) Schema Theory and Related Perspectives

Some cognitive psychologists in the early 1980s focused on text processing as related to readers' prior knowledge. Adults bring prior knowledge to their reading, often extremely well-organized prior knowledge. An adult's associations are not random, but rather similar to the associations of others in his or her culture. From Kennebunkport to Fisherman's Wharf, the word *apple* reliably elicits the associations "orange," "red," and "fruit," and reminds people of the rhyme, "An apple a day keeps the doctor away." The hierarchy of categories in one American adult's head is often similar to that of his or her neighbor, so all of us know about cats and dogs as animals, which are a subset of living things, which is a subset of all things. More complex relationships are also encoded in our prior knowledge, so that many people know about the elements and events that comprise a ship's christening or a visit to a fancy restaurant or a birthday party. R. C. Anderson and Pearson (1984) referred to such knowledge of complex events as schematic.

The schema for a ship christening includes its purpose—to bless the ship. It includes information about where it is done (i.e., in dry dock), by whom (i.e., a celebrity), and when it occurs (i.e., just before launching of a new ship). The christening action (i.e., breaking a bottle of champagne that is suspended from a rope) is also represented in prior knowledge. These parts of a schema are referred to as *nodes, variables*, or *slots*. At any particular christening, these slots are *instantiated* with particular instances (e.g., it occurs at New Haven, with the President or First Lady breaking a bottle of California-produced champagne on a particular new submarine). There are clear constraints on the instances that can occur in these slots. For example, the celebrity would never be a person of ill repute (e.g., a convicted criminal, a publisher of pornography).

schematic processing

Once some small part of the ship christening schema is encountered (e.g., by the image in a news clip of a bottle of champagne breaking on the bow of a ship) the entire schema is activated. Once activated, processing and comprehension of the ship christening event will be different.

Schematic processing is decidedly top-down processing in that once activation of higher order ideas occur, thinking about the details of the situation is constrained. The activated schema will permit reasonable inferences to be made about details of the event (e.g., as the bottle is seen breaking on the bough, the viewer might infer that there was a platform beside the ship with one or more persons on it, one of them a celebrity) and affect the allocation of attention to events associated with the christening (e.g., to the celebrity, to the name of the ship).

Not one, but a number of schema theories have been proposed by cognitive psychologists since the 1970s. Their common thread is that a number of concepts that commonly co-occur in particular situations are related to one another in orderly systems of procedures and expectations. According to schema theories, events and situations have skeleton structures that are pretty much constant, although the particular ways the skeleton takes on flesh varies from instance to instance. For example, Minsky (1975, p. 212) proposed *frame theory*: A frame is a data structure for representing a stereotyped situation, like being in a certain

frame theory

living room, or going to a child's birthday party. Attached to each frame are several kinds of information. Some of this information is about how to use the frame. Some is about what one can expect to happen next. Some is about what to do if these expectations are not confirmed. We can think of a frame as a network of nodes and relations. The "top levels" of a frame are fixed, and represent things that are always true about the supposed situation. The lower levels have many *terminals*—"slots" that must be filled by specific instances or data. Each terminal can specify conditions that its assignment must meet. Simple conditions are specified by markers that might require a terminal assignment to be a person or an object of sufficient value. More complex conditions can specify relations among the things assigned to several terminals.

Consider the birthday party frame (Minsky, 1975). There are certain objects that are always present and actions that always occur at a birthday party. For example, the attendees wear clothes, they bring presents, and games are played. Associated with each of the parts of the fixed frame are constraints on how the frame can be filled out: (a) the clothes are usually Sunday best, although simply good clothes sometimes are acceptable; (b) the present must be something that the birthday child would like to receive and it is bought and presented in birthday gift wrap; (c) there are a set of acceptable games, such as hide-and-seek or pin the tail on the donkey.

Schank and Abelson (1977) also sought to explain the common knowledge that people in a culture possess about recurring complex situations. They proposed that much of knowledge is represented in scripts. Although frames can be used to describe sequences of events, for a number of reasons that need not concern us here, scripts perform the same function, but more thoroughly. Script-like representation of a sequence is an important human ability, because there are many recurring sequences of events in life. For example, there is a sequence of events every time you go to a movie theatre, including traveling to the theatre, buying the ticket, buying some food or beverage, giving the ticket to an usher, finding a seat, watching the film, leaving the seat and heading for the exit, dropping the food wrappers or paper cups in the trash can near the exit, and leaving the building.

Although both frame and script theories have been important in cognitive psychology, *schema theory*, as developed by Richard Anderson and his colleagues at the Illinois Center for the Study of Reading (e.g., R. C. Anderson & Pearson, 1984), has had much more impact in the area of text processing and thus, we discuss this perspective in the remainder of this section. According to schema theory, activation of schemata will occur as concepts are encountered in a text. These will permit prediction of what might occur in the text. Such schemata will also permit inferences. Thus, if the schema for a zoo is activated by the title of a text (e.g., "A Zoo Birthday"), the reader will have expectations about what types of animals will occur in the tale, as well as beliefs about the setting (e.g., there are cages or man-made viewscapes, people come to look at the animals, the people are safe from the animals). The activated schema will also permit appropriate inferences. Thus, if the reader encounters the sentence, "The animals are noisy when the sun rises," the reader may infer that seals bark or lions roar in the morning, but would be less likely to imagine a rooster crowing, a cow mooing, a dog barking, or a house cat meowing. The simultaneous activation of zoo and birthday schemata would also affect how attention is directed in the passage, with readers particularly alert to information about birthdays. Thus, a sentence about a very fat lioness seeking isolation from other lions would receive more attention in a story about birthdays than if the title of the story was, "A Day at the Zoo."

The think-aloud reports summarized in chapter 3 are consistent with schema theory. For certain, many of the think-aloud studies refer to schema theory as a model underlying the development of the study. Sometimes readers explicitly attempt to activate prior knowledge before reading by skimming a text. Sometimes this leads to predictions about text content, consistent with schema theory. Information in text related to schema-based expectations receives differential attention. Consistent with schema theory, when the text contains information congruent with prior knowledge, readers in the think-aloud studies reported that expectations were substantiated. In contrast, when information inconsistent with activated schema was encountered, readers in the think-aloud studies sometimes reported shifting expectations about text meaning to reflect the information presented in the text.

Monitoring the novelty of ideas in text is permitted by well-developed prior knowledge as well as according to schema theory. Consistent with this tenet of schema theory, readers in the think-aloud studies reported awareness of when ideas in text were consistent with prior knowledge and when they were inconsistent with it. Many other evaluations made by readers in the think-aloud studies also reflected prior knowledge, such as decisions to believe or not believe the information in a text.

As was the case for reader response theory and the Baker and Brown (1984) perspective, however, verbal report data demonstrate a great deal of conscious processing during reading that is not well accounted for by schema theory or even by prior knowledge processes in general. For example, there are many strategies besides prediction that are commonly reported by readers as they think aloud. There is also monitoring of much more by readers than whether the information in text is consistent with prior knowledge (e.g., linguistic characteristics of text). Our perspective, informed by the detailed summary of conscious reading processes in chapter 3, acknowledges the importance of prior knowledge in skilled reading, although it suggests that much reading is not so completely knowledge driven. In contrast, the next theory considered emphasizes much more the bottom-up development of meaning during text processing.

Van Dijk and Kintsch's Theory of Discourse Comprehension

Van Dijk and Kintsch (1983) proposed that the meaning of a text begins at the word level, then proceeds to the understanding of clauses that include words, which proceeds to the understanding of sentences, and then to overall text meaning. Throughout the process, however, there is movement back and forth between levels, so that word level processing affects the emerging understanding of the overall text, but the emergent overall understanding also affects comprehension of subsequent words. Thus, encountering the words *lion, tiger,* and *seal,* affects the creation of the overall meaning of a story about a zoo. Once the overall zoo theme is constructed, however, new words are processed differently than they might be otherwise. Thus, the detection of the word *cow* in a story, one that seems to the reader (based on text read until this point) to be about a zoo, might not conjure up images of a barnyard, but result in a search of prior knowledge about what female animals at the zoo are referred to as cows.

According to van Dijk and Kintsch's (1983) model, the starting point for text comprehension is individual words and propositions (i.e., propositions are the most basic relational meaning units in text; e.g., noun–action–noun structures). Propositions in turn are related to one another in text. For example, the sentence, "John hit the big red ball," contains the propositions that "John hit the ball," "The ball is red," and "The ball is big," with these three propositions related to one another in one sentence. As the text is understood, the reader constructs a mental model of the situation represented by the text. That is, the reader comes to understand the events, characters, and actions represented in the text. Thus, the reader may come to imagine John as a little boy batting around a big, red plastic ball with his fist. Of course, this model of the situation is affected both by the elements of text and the reader's prior knowledge, with the reader actively relating prior knowledge to elements in the text as they are encountered. Thus, Pressley's mental model for John hitting the big, red ball was affected by memories of his own son's penchant for bopping a red ball when the family visited the beach a few summers back.

Although readers process much of the meaning represented in text, they do not remember everything. What they tend to remember are the main ideas and how the mains ideas relate to one another, if a focus on main ideas is compatible with the task at hand. Van Dijk and Kintsch (1983) referred to this interrelation of ideas as the *macrostructure*. The construction of the macrostructure occurs throughout reading, beginning with guesses based on words and a few propositions.

As the years have passed, Kintsch (e.g., 1988; Weaver & Kintsch, 1991) has emphasized additionally the bottom-up nature of his framework. Words and propositions relate to the reader's prior knowledge, which produces associations to the words and propositions. Because any word can have a variety of meanings, the one that is favored in any particular context is the one related to other concepts and propositions that are activated currently because they have been encountered in text. Thus, many associations are implicit to the phrase, "The fishing expedition," with only a subset of them remaining active once the proposition, "engaged in by the district attorney," is encountered. If the propositions "in July" and "to the polar region" were encountered, a different set of meaning elements associated with "fishing expedition" would remain active.

Is the van Dijk and Kintsch (1983) framework supported by the think-alouds? As with the theories reviewed earlier in this chapter, the answer is yes, as far as the theory goes. There are reports of explicit attention to individual words and propositions in the think-aloud protocols, as well as reports of construction of macropropositions (i.e., summaries). Readers report attempting to visualize the situations depicted in texts they are reading, consistent with van Dijk and Kintsch's (1983) notion that readers construct situation models. Consistent with van Dijk and Kintsch (1983) are the many reports of understanding parts of text by relating them to prior knowledge.

Much that is salient in think-aloud reports, however, is not accounted for in the van Dijk and Kintsch (1983) model. For example, readers engage in extensive and salient monitoring and evaluation processes as they read. The van Dijk and Kintsch (1983) model is silent on the saliency of such self-reports, with monitoring of comprehension portrayed largely as a by-product of macroproduction construction in their framework (i.e., if a macroproduction occurs, the reader perceives that the text must be understood). Although van Dijk and Kintsch (1983) acknowledged that both top-down and bottom-up processing occur, their strong emphasis on induction of meaning from text is not consistent with the emphatic reports of readers in the think-aloud studies of making predictions about text meaning based on prior knowledge and then either substantiating or revising their expectations. In general, reader attempts to overview text before reading and consciously activate higher order meaning structures (e.g., schemata) that might predict upcoming content are also not consistent with van Dijk and Kintsch's (1983) perspective on meaning construction. Van Dijk and Kintsch (1983) provided detailed explanation of strategies that permit construction of macropropositions: For example, they focused on readers exploiting knowledge of text structure and syntactic structures to create meaning. They also emphasized deletion and generalization strategies that permit reduction of many micropropositions to a single macroproposition. Nonetheless, their framework is silent with respect to most other strategies that readers use. That is, there is more in the think-aloud protocols than the critical strategies highlighted by van Dijk and Kintsch (1983). Again, although the van Dijk and Kintsch (1983) model has informed the development of a number of verbal report studies, verbal report studies in aggregate describe many more processes, as summarized in chapter 3.

Models of Text Inferential Processes

Based on prior knowledge, people often construct inferences that go beyond the information presented in text (for reviews, see Balota, d'Arcais, & Rayner, 1990; Graesser & Bower, 1990). This inference making is an important part of meaning construction. Many types of inferences can be made, and many types have been studied by researchers to date: causal, thematic, spatial, temporal, logical, lexical, and anaphoric (see Graesser & Kreuz, 1993; Kintsch, 1993; van den Broek, Fletcher, & Risden, 1993).

A variety of sensitive experimental procedures (methods not necessary to understand in this context) are being used by cognitive psychologists to explore when inferences occur during reading and to construct models of inferential meaning construction during text processing. What these experiments have established is that some types of inferences seem to occur on-line more reliably than others, including the following (see Graesser & Kreuz, 1993):

1. Pronoun referents, especially when the referent was recently presented in text (e.g., "When I threw the ball, it hit him on the head," results in *ball* being inferred as the referent of *it*).

2. Superordinate goals, such as when a reader encounters, "The man nodded approvingly to the clerk when he brought out the Rolex and took out his check book," and infers that the man is shopping for a watch (e.g., Long & Golding, 1993; Long, Golding, & Graesser, 1992; Trabasso & Suh, 1993).

3. Causal antecedents (i.e., a bridging inference from a currently encountered piece of information to information presented earlier explaining the currently processed content; e.g., van den Broek, 1990a, 1990b; van den Broek & Lorch, 1993).

Evidence for other types of inferences has been obtained much less reliably in the experimental studies, with many inferences seeming to depend on a number of situational factors (Graesser & Kreuz, 1993; van den Broek et al., 1993) including the type of text, the text processor's orientation to the text (e.g., the intent to read carefully and understand completely increases the likelihood of inferences), the criterion task the processor expects (e.g., preparing to generate a summary seems to stimulate inferential integration), and processor characteristics (e.g., high prior knowledge of a text's topic and large working-memory capacity are associated with greater inferencing).

The think-aloud data support the conclusion that inferencing occurs during reading, with evidence for many types of conscious inferences in the think-aloud reports. The think-alouds are particularly rich with information about processes that contribute to inference making, such as the reports of different ways to integrate across different parts of text in order to understand fully. To date, think-aloud data have not been analyzed in an attempt to determine whether they elucidate when inferences might be expected and when they are less likely, however, which has been a main concern of the cognitive science experimentalists interested in inference. That there are so many conscious processes represented in the think-alouds that seem to relate to inference, however, suggests that the predominant tactic in the experimental literature of attempting to determine whether an inference occurred or not is but part of the picture. Verbal reports provide information on both the varied processes used by readers and the products they yield. Thus, whether the think-alouds support the particular models of inference that have been tested seems less important than that the think-alouds support the conclusion that reading is massively inferential. However, because reading consists of many other elements (e.g., strategy, monitoring, evaluation) it is clear that the theories of inferential comprehension are only an important slice of the full array of processes that constitute skilled reading.

Sociocultural Theories of Reading

How is reading a social act when a reader reads a text, and how is reading used socially once the reader understands the text? Our goal for this section is not to add to sociocultural theories of reading (e.g., Beach & Hynds, 1991; Fish, 1980;

Flower, 1987; Holland, 1975) or to test the theories with verbal report data. This is a relatively new area of focus for think-aloud studies and the existing verbal report data are intriguing. But we are not sure that the data are ready to bear more than the weight of the suggestion that this is a rich and promising area.

Geisler (1991) noted the importance of examining acts of literacy as they occur "at the axis of individual cognition and the axis of social interaction" (p. 171). Expert readers regularly demonstrate these social dimensions of reading, and we see threads of sociocultural theories of reading in several of the models we previously considered. Our examination of the expert reader suggests that often a conversation is developed between the reader and the perceived author. This conversation is social and interpersonal by nature, and it is anticipated by both cognitive psychology and reader response theories. The social act of responding to an author while reading the author's text is clearly tied to reader response theories, as a reader's possession and use of prior knowledge of author's intent, or prior knowledge of the content of the text, is accommodated by cognitive theory.

Johnston and Afflerbach (1985) and Afflerbach (1990b) were informative about sociocultural influences on reading. Their subjects' expertise in a particular knowledge domain appeared to influence the nature of readers' cognitive processes as well as their reports of how the meaning constructed (or constructed and refuted) might be used with other people. Subjects included anthropology professors as well as doctoral students in anthropology and chemistry. Those with extensive prior knowledge sometimes mentally engaged the author of the text; for example, suggesting the author's implicit purpose. Sometimes subjects would recommend additional reading for the author! Readers with less prior knowledge of a domain were sometimes reduced to a position of blind faith in the author. That is, lacking knowledge to read critically, readers were placed in a position of constructing received knowledge (Belenky, Clinchy, Goldberger, & Tarule, 1986). These readers were parties to a forced social contract with the author of the text they were reading: They had some faith that they were not being misled or misinformed, but they had no means of determining if their faith was well placed, or misplaced. This was an extreme version of the Gricean principle (Grice, 1989) that readers and authors expect the best from one another.

Wineberg's (1991) historians understood not only the history texts they read, but the subtexts of the texts. This ability allowed historians to infer an author's values, intent, and level of domain knowledge. Wineberg noted that competent readers may have very plausible reasons for being slow and careful readers of texts that relate to their field of expertise. An historian reading an account of familiar events, persons, and settings may have much to process: affect related to text content and author style, domain prior knowledge that meshes or contrasts with the author's, and a conversational refutation or salutation for the absent author. The reader may also be occupied with imagining a future conversation with a colleague, an important point to make in an upcoming seminar, or an addition to an evolving article that the reader is writing. In this case, the rate of reading is not determined exclusively by readers' cognitive process or prowess: it is also determined by current and anticipated social uses of what is read.

We also found examples of the social aspect of expert reading in the work of Haas and Flower (1988). They reported readers who were active in constructing an understanding of author purpose, and constructing the context in which a text was written (and the context that the author envisioned the text would be read in). The readers also reported imagining how other readers would read and react to the text. Finally, Geisler (1991) found that expert readers inferred an author's intention or purpose; subsequently, they sometimes engaged in the social acts of dismissing not only the premise of a text, but the work of the author who produced the text.

Unfortunately, a distinct minority of the verbal report studies we analyzed drew from sociocultural perspectives on reading and literacy. However, because readers often related what they read to people they knew and to social uses, it is clear that reading is socially embedded. We found ourselves wishing, however, that researchers in this area would have generated data telling about whether thinking about literature is the same in groups as it is for individuals (although see Beach, 1972, for an interesting analysis that did so). We also found ourselves wishing that there were studies addressing whether it makes a difference if one is reading in anticipation of interacting with others about a reading or reading only to self-inform. Notably, some of the fullest reports we encountered in our review of the literature were generated in Kintgen's (1983) study, in which readers were asked to prepare for a group discussion, suggesting that such a demand may really encourage in-depth reading and thinking. Of course, given that there was no manipulation of the demand in the study, we cannot be certain whether the richness of the protocols were because of the demands, the types of readers, or the types of text. We need true experimentation aimed at illuminating the question of whether reading with the goal of interacting with others about text content shapes thinking during reading.

Summary

All of the models reviewed in this section have contributed to our evolving understanding of skilled reading. Indeed, many of the models reviewed here had a visible hand in the development and conducting of subsequent verbal report studies. Yet none of the models alone can account for the rich mix of strategies, monitoring, and evaluative processes that constitute skilled reading as depicted in chapter 3.

When the summary in chapter 3 is considered, it is clear that all of the perspectives represented in the models considered in this section must be included in a comprehensive model of text processing. Although all of the theories reviewed in this section are on target, none of them go far enough. We propose an alternative in the next section of this chapter that captures all of the processes considered by these previous models, one based on the analyses summarized in chapter 3.

CONSTRUCTIVELY RESPONSIVE READING

captures all of the processes [handwritten]

constructive Theorists [handwritten]

We continue here a theme begun in chapter 3, that skilled reading is constructive reading in the sense of traditional constructivist theorists, from Piaget, Vygotsky, and Bruner, to those who have thought about the constructive nature of education and reading in light of modern research and data (e.g., Chan, Burtis, Scardamalia, & Bereiter, 1992; Moshman, 1982; Poplin, 1988a, 1988b; Pressley, Harris, & Marks, 1992). The telltale signs of reader construction of meaning in the think-aloud protocols included the following:

signs of reader construction of meaning [handwritten]

1. Many readers in the think-aloud studies clearly were determined to get the overall meaning of the texts they were reading through active search and reflection.

2. Inaccuracies in meaning construction are reported on the way to understanding, with the errors often reflecting interpretations based on prior knowledge; that the pursuit of more adequate understanding continues even after initial interpretations based on prior knowledge are made reflects awareness of potential differences between the meaning of the text and the conjectured meaning based on prior knowledge.

3. The reading in the protocol studies often was passionate and engaged.

4. The self-reports revealed that what the readers knew before reading the text predicted to some extent their eventual processing of it.

In making the claim that reading is constructivist, we focus greatly on the activities of the reader. What must not be forgotten is that whenever there is a reader, there is also a text, and the text in part determines the activities of the reader: readers react to text. Hence, what we propose here as a summary of skilled reading is a model of constructively responsive reading.

To do so, we create what some might consider a convenient fiction—a reader who potentially could carry out all of the reading strategies and processes summarized in chapter 3. Even if such a composite reader does not exist, we are confident, based on our review of some of the more complete summaries of exceptionally skilled reading covered in chapter 3, that there are approximations to such an ideal constructively responsive reader. Thus, we believe that there are many readers who are constructively responsive as we describe here, especially when they are working with texts that are important to them, interesting to them, and related to matters in which they have decidedly well-informed opinions and clear expertise.

ideal reader [handwritten]

In offering this conception of reading, we also recognize that there are many different goals that can motivate reading of a text and that constructively responsive reading is going to be different depending on the reader's goal. We note, however, that most think-aloud analyses involved careful reading of text, because the primary reader goal in most studies was either to learn the material in the text or, at least, understand it. Thus, in what follows, we assume that the constructively responsive reader is reading for fairly complete understanding of text (i.e., reading carefully), the type of understanding that would permit recall of at least the most important themes of the text sometime after reading is concluded. When all four tell-tale signs are considered, the case is overwhelming that the reading summarized in chapter 3 was constructively responsive.

what is goal — purpose affect reading strategies

Tell-Tale Sign Number One: Readers Seek Overall Meaning of Text, Actively Searching, Reflecting On, and Responding to Text in Pursuit of Main Ideas

seeks main ideas

The skilled reader comes to a text knowing that it has main ideas. The good reader also knows that much of reading is construction of macropropositions, to use van Dijk and Kintsch's (1983) term. There are many strategies for getting such big points, with many think-aloud remarks reflecting the search for main ideas.

The search for main ideas can begin with a reader's overview of the text. The overview can provide a great deal of information about the general type of information covered in the text and where various topics in the reading are located. It is not unusual for the skilled reader to emerge from such an overview with initial hypotheses about the main ideas in the reading. These initial hypotheses will be held in mind and evaluated as reading begins. There is definitely differential attention to information in text that seems centrally relevant. Additional predictions are made in response to ideas encountered as the text unfolds. Old predictions are sometimes discarded or updated in reaction to what is encountered during the careful reading of the text. The reader sometimes jumps back and forth to carefully consider important points in the text, points that seem critical to comprehend in order to get the gist of the text.

overview. search for initial hypotheses

Consistent with constructivist thinking, there is some tension in such reading between focus on the parts of the text and construction of the whole meaning. The construction of macropropositions requires comprehension and the support of many micropropositions. Insufficient attention to details that are the micropropositions may preclude the development of some important macropropositions. Thus, many of the strategies of skilled reading that reflect concern with details are essential to main idea construction. It is evident, however, from the summarizing and highlighting of main ideas in the verbal protocols that the skilled reader does not lose track of the pursuit of the main idea.

✓ looking for details as well as main ideas)

Inferential activities also reflect the pursuit of larger themes, from inferences about the author's overall intent in writing the piece to the drawing of conclusions strongly implied by the text. Readers' awareness that the parts of text add up to a much greater whole is reflected by their many attempts to integrate across disparate parts of readings. Those attempts also reflect determination to get at the larger meaning of text, for protocol study participants reported great efforts expended in comparing parts of text, holding disparate ideas in working memory while searching for related ideas throughout text, and rereading to clarify how previously encountered information related to parts of text just covered.

After a text has been read, additional reflection and rereading are common, again in the service of finding the larger meaning of the text. Readers monitor whether they have comprehended a reading. If they feel they have not comprehended the text's overall meaning, this can be motivation to process the text additionally and/or differently in order to construct a more complete understanding of it. Evaluations of the whole text are common in reader remarks, including evaluations of the validity, interestingness, structural integrity, and sophistication of the overall text.

In short, there were many indications in the think-alouds that readers pursue and reflect on the overall meanings of the texts they are reading. They do so by reflecting on and integrating across details, however. Their responses to details often reflect perceptions of the importance of details to the main theme (e.g., skipping a part of text that is tangential to the main ideas of a piece, scrutinizing a part of the text that is important to the theme of the text). As readers construct the main ideas from the bits and pieces of meaning they encounter in text, they also reflect on and respond to these constructions, modifying them when information in the text is inconsistent with the emerging macroproposition or reacting by additional reading and study of the text. There is construction and response throughout the process of reading for understanding, with pursuit of an understanding of the whole stimulating much processing and analysis of the parts of text.

Tell-Tale Sign Number Two: Readers Respond to Text with Predictions and Hypotheses That Reflect Their Prior Knowledge

The knowledge a person brings to a text is a powerful determinant of text comprehension. Often, however, a reader will depart a text knowing something different than what they expected to know as a function of reading the text or what they knew previously. Prior knowledge is a powerful source of hypotheses, hypotheses that are tested and refined as the text is processed. Good readers are very aware of the mismatches in their expectations about text meaning and claims that can be defended based on information in the text when they occur, with this awareness reflected in the think-aloud data.

When readers overview text, they are attempting to get an idea about what the text is about, with hypotheses advanced about the potential meaning of the text. Hypothesis generation continues as front-to-back reading begins. At some point, information will be encountered making clear that at least some of the hypothesized points are in error, as when Phillips' (1988) one reader suddenly realized that hypotheses about sailors were wrong. This realization came when information about fishing nets was encountered, making clear that the story was about fishermen rather than sailors.

Is there anything dysfunctional about generating inaccurate predictions? Not from the perspective of constructivism. They reflect active engagement, attempts to understand text by relating it to prior knowledge. That such errors were common in the think-alouds makes clear the constructive nature of the reading captured in the protocol analyses. That the initial hypotheses of the readers did not prevail but yielded to information in the text makes clear the responsive nature of skilled reading. The hypothesis refinements evident in the protocols are strong evidence that the reading summarized in chapter 3 is both reflectively constructive and responsive.

Tell-Tale Sign Number Three: Readers Are Passionate in Their Responses to Text

Passionate reading was more evident in some of the protocol analyses than in others. In particular, it was more apparent in studies involving readers with great expertise, especially when they were reading texts that were definitely interesting to them. These included Afflerbach's (1990b) study of doctoral students in anthropology reading an article about native American arrowheads; Bazerman's (1985) physicists reading physics articles of their own selection; Charney's (1993) study of ecologists, a paleontologist, and an anthropologist reading an article attacking evolutionary biology; Lundeberg's (1987) evaluation of law professors and attorneys reading legal cases; Shearer et al.'s (1993) analysis of teachers reading articles concerned with teaching; and Wyatt et al.'s (1993) study of social scientists reading articles pertinent to their work.

At one level, the passion is evident in how much these readers report reading. For example, Bazerman (1985), Shearer et al. (1993), and Wyatt et al. (1993) confirmed that their readers were active in seeking out professional material to read. There was plenty of evidence of passion within the protocols as well, however, with much of it classified as evaluation. Readers did not hesitate to point out their approval and disapproval of ideas in text, the strength of arguments, the validity of evidence, and the author's style and modus operandi. There was surprise, laughter, puzzlement, frustration, and anxiety in the think-aloud reports. These responses were possible because of the extensive prior knowledge and the related values and beliefs of the readers in these studies.

Consider Wyatt et al.'s (1993) detailed report about the passions of one reader, a science educator. At one point the reader responded to the article he was reading, "Not only that, so this thing does not measure the impact of conceptual knowledge, but then they sort of ignored the treatment. And the treatment they do is fairly terrible" (p. 62). As the reading continues, the reader's responses increase in negativity: "And it sort of gets me angry that we don't use better instruments" (p. 63). And as far as this reader's overall evaluation, his disgust with the article comes through with his summary, "Well, that's baloney" (p. 63). Moreover, this reader's reactions were fairly typical of the passions observed by Wyatt et al. (1993) as they watched 15 social scientists read text: Eight of their 15 definitely expressed positive affect at the messages they encountered in the texts they read; 11 expressed surprise; 9 of 15 were obviously bored; and 9 of 15 were so negatively impressed by the content of the text that they swore about it!!

The passionate responses are constructive in the sense that the reader's prior knowledge filtered the information presented in the text, heightening attention to content that is responded to emotionally. The passion is responsive in that it was elicited by particular points in text. When constructively responsive readers process texts related to their prior understandings and interests, they are likely either to embrace the messages in text, reject them, or possibly embrace some points and reject others. At least some of the protocol analyses summarized in chapter 3 were sensitive to passionate reader responses.

Tell-Tale Sign Number Four: Readers' Prior Knowledge Predicts Their Comprehension Processing and Responses to Text

Perhaps the most critical claim of constructivist theories is that what one knows already largely determines what ones learns given new information. Consistent with this tenet of constructivism, the effects of prior knowledge are apparent in many ways in protocols of skilled reading.

While overviewing the text, some readers in the protocol studies attempted to activate prior knowledge, for example, through search of their memories for information relevant to the topic of the text they were preparing to read. The initial hypotheses about the meaning of text that result from overviewing are a product of associative responses to information encountered during the preview.

As reading proceeds, additional associative responding based on prior knowledge is common. Also, prior knowledge affects decisions about what is potentially important (e.g., novel) in a text and worthy of differential attention and what is not so worthy. Inferences are largely based on prior knowledge. For example, conjectures about Michener's purpose in writing his current book are informed by knowledge of Michener's purposes in writing previous books. Interpretive categorizations of a work (e.g., a "political satire" or an "historical fiction") require knowledge of such genres. In fact, interpretations of all sorts require prior knowledge that permits the reader to imagine the state of affairs depicted in the text as well as how the state depicted in the text contrasts with other states of affairs. Thus, it is impossible to come to an interpretation of the importance of the Kennedy presidency without knowledge of other presidencies.

As much depends on p.k.: general conventions of reading as well as on any matter

Comprehension monitoring is largely enabled by prior knowledge. Much of deciding whether text is comprehended is based on whether the message abstracted from the text makes sense relative to what the reader already knows about the topic of the text. Monitoring also involves awareness of how the new information relates to old knowledge and whether one's personal prior knowledge permits full appreciation of the text.

Evaluative responses to a text are not possible without massive prior knowledge. Judgments about the qualities of a text depend on knowing a great deal about how texts can be (and typically are) written and about previously existing ideas relevant to the text. Thus, a reviewer for an academic journal can judge fairly the uniqueness of a manuscript submitted for publication only if he or she is armed with knowledge of the previous work related to the piece under review. Readers embrace pieces that are consistent with what they already believe and often reject writing that is filled with information inconsistent with their own views of the world.

to know what something is ? have know what it isn't.

is this contradictory

Thus, what one knows already affects what one is prepared to find in a text, with the reader who is high in prior knowledge of a text's domain better prepared to spot important information in a new article. Such knowledge can help to shape one's interpretations of the content in a new article as well as affect whether the article is held in high esteem or dismissed. High prior knowledge can also promote tunnel vision. Prior knowledge affects meaning construction processes in many ways, although the meaning that results from reading a text develops in response to the particular points made in the text. A reader's understanding of a text reflects both his or her prior knowledge and responses to information presented in the text, with many of the responses determined largely by prior knowledge.

Summary

Constructivist theorists believe that humans are extremely active in their pursuit of meaning. New information is not simply received, but rather humans construct hypotheses about the meaning of new information and test those hypotheses against the subsequent input. Humans filter new information through prior knowledge, elaborating the new ideas by relating them to what is already known. (For a general summary of this constructivist model of learning, see Driscoll, 1994, chapter 11).

We trust that our detailed analysis of verbal report data in chapter 3 conveys a strong impression that extremely active reading was observed in the think-aloud studies. Hypothesis formation and testing is common as part of pursuing the meaning of text. The filtering of text-based ideas through prior knowledge is apparent during monitoring and especially in reader evaluations, with readers ready to reject text-based ideas inconsistent with their prior knowledge and approve of ideas that are sensible based on what they know already. It is easy to recognize the Piagetian constructive processes of assimilation and accommodation in the think-aloud protocols, with assimilation obvious when text meaning is shaped by prior knowledge and accommodation apparent when readers' ideas

I wonder how much meaning is rejected?

about the meaning of text shift as new information in text is encountered. Some ideas in text are simply added to prior knowledge; others ideas in text require that prior knowledge be fine tuned; still, other ideas result in prior knowledge being restructured to accommodate the new-to-the-reader perspective expressed in the text, consistent with constructivist models of knowing (e.g., Rumelhart & Norman, 1975, 1978).

One important tenet of constructivism is that learning is likely to be best in the context of meaningful activity (e.g., Driscoll, 1994). Thus, it perhaps is not surprising that some of the most interesting and complete reports of text processing occurred in studies in which readers were reading material related to their work and interests, such as when physicists read physics, teachers read articles about teaching, and social scientists read social science. Reading is embedded in a life context. Another tenet is that thinking is reflectively critical, that there is mindful consideration of the information in text. Again, although reflection and mindfulness were common in the think-alouds, high levels of awareness and thoughtful consideration of text meaning were especially apparent when people were reading texts strongly related to their prior knowledge and interests.

reading is embedded in a life context

Constructivists emphasize that humans attempt to understand wholes, although, paradoxically, this often requires detailed analysis of parts (e.g., Poplin, 1988a, 1988b). Throughout the protocols, there is clearly greater attention to acquiring an overall understanding of text than worrying about details, although details definitely elicit responses (e.g., individual words are pondered, especially if they are not understood at first).

Expert readers are social animals. In addition to the specific requests and directions made by researchers, many expert readers clearly place their reading in a self-determined context. The context may be near (the social interactions of a reader giving verbal reports with a researcher present), or removed (the reader's anticipated uses of what is being read and the people who may be involved in these interactions). From this perspective, cognition and response during reading are a midpoint on the path that a reader takes from beginning the reading of a text to using what is understood from the text.

In conclusion, the composite reader who emerges from the chapter 3 summary is after the big ideas in text. This reader comes to the task with some general tendencies: for example, to overview the text as a way to begin understanding it and to plan reading of the text; to read from the front to the end of the text in general, but to veer off this course when comprehension requires processing of information found elsewhere in the text; to use strategies (or moves, as some authors refer to them; e.g., Lytle, 1982) in coming to terms with text, including predicting, visualizing, summarizing, rereading as needed, and so on; to monitor comprehension and other aspects of reading as part of the strategic planning process that continues throughout the reading; and to relate the information in text to prior knowledge, permitting both formation of hypotheses about the meaning of the text and evaluations of the text and the hypotheses. How these

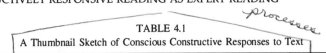

TABLE 4.1

A Thumbnail Sketch of Conscious Constructive Responses to Text

- Overviewing before reading (determining what is there and deciding which parts to process).
- Looking for important information in text and paying greater attention to it than other information (e.g., adjusting reading speed and concentration depending on the perceived importance of text to reading goals).
- Attempting to relate important points in text to one another in order to understand the text as a whole.
- Activating and using prior knowledge to interpret text (generating hypotheses about text, predicting text content).
- Relating text content to prior knowledge, especially as part of constructing interpretations of text.
- Reconsidering and/or revising hypotheses about the meaning of text based on text content.
- Reconsidering and/or revising prior knowledge based on text content.
- Attempting to infer information not explicitly stated in text when the information is critical to comprehension of the text.
- Attempting to determine the meaning of words not understood or recognized, especially when a word seems critical to meaning construction.
- Using strategies to remember text (underlining, repetition, making notes, visualizing, summarizing, paraphrasing, self-questioning, etc.).
- Changing reading strategies when comprehension is perceived not to be proceeding smoothly.
- Evaluating the qualities of text, with these evaluations in part affecting whether text has impact on reader's knowledge, attitudes, behavior, and so on.
- Reflecting on and processing text additionally after a part of text has been read or after a reading is completed (reviewing, questioning, summarizing, attempting to interpret, evaluating, considering alternative interpretations and possibly deciding between them, considering how to process the text additionally if there is a feeling it has not been understood as much as it needs to be understood, accepting one's understanding of the text, rejecting one's understanding of a text).
- Carrying on responsive conversation with the author.
- Anticipating or planning for the use of knowledge gained from the reading.

general tendencies play out depends largely on the nature of the text. That is, the general meaning construction tendencies of the skilled reader are shaped into specific responses to a particular text largely by specific characteristics of the text and information in it. The reader's constructive tendencies and responses to text determine the type of meaning construction and, ultimately, the meaning that is finally arrived at, a point we continue to develop in the next section in which constructively responsive reading is analyzed in terms of expert theory. As an *aide memoire* of the many processes that comprise constructive responsivity, we offer Table 4.1.

CONSTRUCTIVELY RESPONSIVE READING AS EXPERT READING

Since the 1970s, cognitive psychologists have expended considerable effort explicating the nature of expert performance, with studies of diverse experts (i.e., from radiologists to chess players; see Chi, Glaser, & Farr, 1988) yielding generally consistent portraits of expertise. Some of the generalizations about expertise that have been produced in this body of literature (Glaser & Chi, 1988; Lesgold et al., 1988) include that experts:

- excel mainly in their own domains.
- perceive large meaningful patterns in their domains of competence.
- have superior short-term memory.
- see and represent problems in their domain at a deeper (more principled) level than novices; novices tend to represent problems at a superficial level.
- devote considerable effort to planning their thinking.
- can efficiently carry out a variety of skills required in their domain.
- can self-monitor well.
- are opportunistic, making use of whatever information is available and useful.

To the extent that comparisons between more and less expert readers are possible from the literature summarized in Table 4.1, the comparisons support the conclusion that better and more experienced readers (e.g., more experienced with the domain covered in the text they are reading) are more capably and certainly constructively responsive than weaker and less experienced readers; that better and/or more experienced readers in a domain are more expert in their reading than weaker and/or less experienced readers in a domain. Consider the following examples:

- Deegan (1993) observed that first-year law students who were doing well in law school read differently than first-year law students experiencing difficulties in school. Specifically, the better students were more likely to respond to text with questions about the meaning and structure of a law-related text that they read.

- When Earthman (1989) had both graduate students in English and college freshmen read short stories and poems, she found that the graduate students were more likely than freshmen to work at filling in gaps in meaning in the texts and were more likely to relate texts to knowledge of the world. The graduate students were also more likely to take alternative perspectives while reading the literary works.

- Graves and Frederiksen (1991) observed considerable differences between the think-alouds of English professors reading an excerpt from *The Color Purple* and college sophomores doing so: The professors were more aware of the functions of the narrative in the text as well as the relationship of the author to the reader of the text. The experts viewed the text as the result of deliberate choices made by the author, with their perceptions of these choices affecting their understanding of the text.

• Haas and Flowers (1988) observed that graduate students were more likely than undergraduate students to do "rhetorical reading" of a section of an undergraduate textbook. That is, they attempted to understand the author's intentions in writing the text as it was written.

• Hare (1981) reported that good compared to weaker college student readers were more likely to monitor their comprehension as they read and set into motion fixup strategies when comprehension was less than complete.

• Lundeberg (1987) observed that legal experts were more likely than legal novices to attend to important information in a legal case they read, overview the case, attempt to summarize it, evaluate it, and reread the case analytically.

• In a study of 10th graders, Olshavsky (1976–1977) observed that good readers were more likely than weaker readers to make use of context cues to figure out difficult words and were more likely to construct hypotheses about the meaning of what they read.

• In Phillips' (1988) study of sixth-graders, readers with high proficiency and high background knowledge were more likely than other readers to shift strategies when a comprehension difficulty was encountered, more likely to attempt to verify their emerging interpretations of text meaning, and more likely to empathize with messages in text.

• Pritchard (1990a) studied American and Paluan students as they read texts pertaining to U. S. and Paluan culture. Background knowledge was more certainly applied by readers when they read culturally familiar texts. Extrapolations from text were also more likely when readers were more familiar with the culture described by the text. Coping strategies with unfamiliar texts were not particularly analytical, with simple rereading more common with culturally unfamiliar than familiar texts.

• As Wineberg's (1991) historians read American history textbook material, they were much more likely than high school students to search for the authorial intentions and hidden meanings. High schools students treated the texts more as factual documents containing information that was not open to question—the historians questioned.

In summary, whenever protocol analyses have permitted comparisons between more and less able readers and/or more and less experienced readers in a domain, the more able and/or more domain-experienced readers have been more constructively responsive in their reading than the less able and/or less domain-experienced readers. The expert nature of constructively responsive reading becomes clearer by examining the reading observed in the protocol analyses in light of each characteristic of expertise summarized at the beginning of this section.

Is Constructively Responsive Reading Expert Reading?

An immediate difficulty in considering constructively responsive reading in light of expert theory and data is that the main points about expertise often are offered as comparisons between the performances of experts and novices. The protocol analyses were not designed to provide expert–novice comparisons with respect to any of these characteristics. Thus, often all that we can do is appraise whether the composite reader who emerges from the chapter 3 analysis possesses the characteristic of expertise.

More Evident in a Domain of Expertise. Is constructively responsive reading more likely in an area of expertise than in an area where one does not possess expertise, consistent with expert theory? With the exception of two studies (Afflerbach, 1990b; Pritchard, 1990a), protocol analyses of domain experts have not been conducted in which the readers read both in a domain of competence and another domain. For these two studies, more skilled reading was observed when there was congruence between the text read and the reader's background, although readers remained skilled when they read in a less familiar content domain, trying to compensate for their lack of prior knowledge. More such comparisons need to be carried out to permit a definitive conclusion about whether constructive responsivity is limited to an area of expertise compared to other domains (or at least greater in the area of expertise). Certainly it was the assumption of researchers who have had domain experts read in their disciplines (Afflerbach, 1990b; Bazerman, 1985; Charney, 1993; Deegan, 1993; Graves & Frederiksen, 1991; Lundeberg, 1987; Schwegler & Shamoon, 1991; Shearer et al., 1993; Wineberg, 1991; Wyatt et al., 1993) that the experts would read at an especially high level of proficiency when processing text from a competence domain. Still, it is logically possible that learning to read constructively and critically in one domain would have carry-over effects to other domains. Whether (or how much) constructive responsivity depends on prior knowledge has yet to be determined.

Perception of Large Patterns. When constructively responsive readers overview, they are trying to get an overall impression of text. To the extent that main themes are detected and summarized, there is evidence of large patterns being detected. When readers monitor whether the meaning of a text as a whole is consistent with prior knowledge or evaluate the overall meaning of a text, there is evidence that they have perceived the text globally. In general, there is evidence in the protocols that constructively responsive readers are attempting to read so as to identify the big meanings represented in texts. The literature is less informative about whether they succeed in doing so.

Superior Short-Term Memory. Whether constructively responsive readers have superior short-term memory is difficult to assess. That they must have extensive short-term memory is certain, however, for they carry out many processes that demand high short-term memory. From comparing predicted interpretations with ideas actually represented in the text to integrating over units of text to comparing one portion of text with another, many of the processes included in chapter 3 are short-term capacity demanding.

Deep Representations. There is no doubt that the lawyers in Deegan (1993) and Lundeberg (1987) as well as the physicists in Bazerman (1985), the historians in Wineberg (1991), and the social scientists in Wyatt et al. (1993) had extremely deep representations of the domain-relevant articles they read, offering many conclusions that reflect much more than the ideas expressed in the texts. In general, protocol analysts who have studied domain experts reading in their areas of competence have concluded that experts report much more than superficial understandings as they process texts in their domain.

Planful. Constructively responsive readers spend a substantial portion of total reading time planning how they are going to process the text. They often overview before reading at all. They monitor their ongoing comprehension as part of on-line planning of how to proceed. They develop plans for how they may use their reading in a social context. They reflect on text after reading to determine if they should process it additionally. Constructively responsive readers also have efficient criteria for determining levels of success for a given combination of text and task.

An important characteristic of constructively responsive readers is that they do not adhere slavishly to plans they make. As we expand in a subsequent subsection, constructive responsivity changes as the demands and opportunities become apparent during reading—they really are responsive to the text, rather than adhering to an a priori plan.

Efficient Processing. There were many indicators in the think-aloud data that skilled readers can carry out efficiently the strategic, monitoring, and evaluative processes they elect. Such readers are not trying to figure out what it means to visualize text content or what should be in a summary: They know and can carry out these processes (and many others) with relatively little effort devoted to any one of them, although, of course, the many processes constructively responsive readers elect during reading of a text can amount to a massive effort. Our clear sense is that such complex processing is typically intentional (e.g., Bereiter & Scardamalia, 1989), an extremely mindful (e.g., Saloman & Globerson, 1987) approach to text, even though the individual processes that the intentional, mindful reader employs to make meaning from text are familiar, automatic, and executed individually with little effort.

Efficient and Effective Self-Monitoring. The substantial number of monitoring processes covered in chapter 3 alone attests to the self-monitoring competencies of the constructively responsive reader. As we read the actual protocols,

*self-
monitoring
processes*

we were convinced that the better readers in these studies often seemed to know when they knew and when they did not know. In addition, they monitored construction and response in terms of particular goals that were cognitive and social. Part of reading intentionally is continuing awareness of the relationship of what is being learned from text to the learning goal (Bereiter & Scardamalia, 1989); such monitoring is an excellent indicator of mindfulness during reading, in contrast to mindless automatic reeling off of intellectual processes (Langer, 1989; Saloman & Globerson, 1987).

Opportunistic. There can be little doubt that constructively responsive readers are opportunistic. Indeed, such opportunism is the responsive part of their processing. If they have an overall plan for reading a text (e.g., formulated as a function of overviewing), this plan is not followed rigidly. Rather, constructively responsive readers exploit text clues and their prior knowledge when opportunities arise.

Summary. Constructively responsive reading has many of the characteristics of expert performance. There is definitely a lot of planning as part of reading, consistent with the observation that experts plan extensively before attempting cognitive operations. Although the individual reading processes are each carried out efficiently, constructively responsive reading is short-term capacity demanding, a type of reading requiring the ability to hold a great deal of information in consciousness at one time. Constructively responsive readers monitor their reading and characteristics of the text, with this monitoring undoubtedly contributing to their ability to take advantage of meaning construction opportunities afforded by text.

The origins of expert performance have been analyzed in detail by cognitive psychologists. Thus, what is known about the development of expert performance in general can be a source of hypotheses about the development of particular forms of expertise, such as constructively responsive reading. It can also shed light on educational experiences that might be expected to promote the development of constructively responsive reading.

Hypotheses About the Development of Constructively Responsive Reading

Cognitive psychologists who have studied expertise are in agreement that it requires a great deal of experience to become expert in a domain. For example, great composers and artists did not begin their careers producing great pieces of music and art, but rather worked as composers and artists for a decade or more before great work began to emerge (Hayes, 1985). Chess grandmasters invariably have played the game for 10 or more years (deGroot, 1965, 1966; Simon & Chase, 1973). An expert radiologist has read 200,000 or more x-rays (Lesgold et al., 1988). Outstanding young adult artists, researchers, and athletes invariably have been working in their area of expertise for most of their lives, having been singled-out at an early age for intensive instruction and opportunities in their domain of budding competence (e.g., Bloom, 1985).

If expert theory is applicable to constructively responsive reading, then one important expectation is that full-blown constructively responsive reading would be difficult or impossible for many children and most likely in exceptionally experienced readers. While claiming this, we note also that many young readers may have the foundations on which constructively responsive reading rests, and on which constructively responsive reading can develop. Children who have rich language experiences, who are learning to be mindful as they read, who are persistent in their own attempts to read, who know the social uses of reading, and who approach reading with purpose, humor, creativity, and imagination probably have a shorter path to constructive responsivity than classmates who have underdeveloped language, are not intentionally mindful as they read potentially informative texts, give up on meaning construction when reading becomes difficult, and lack purpose, humor, creativity, and imagination.

Consistent with this analysis, in protocol analyses to date, children have not been nearly as constructively responsive as the most skilled of adult readers. For example, Meyers, Lytle, Palladino, Davenpeck, and Green (1990) observed that students in Grades 5 and 6 signaled their understandings as they read, elaborated, and reasoned about text meaning (i.e., constructed hypotheses about meaning and tested the hypotheses, revising them as needed). Even so, Meyers et al.'s (1990) subjects rarely monitored their understanding, did not evaluate what they read, nor did they analyze the structural or rhetorical characteristics of the text. Kucan (1993) used the same scoring scheme as Meyers et al. (1990). With Grade-6 students, she observed a pattern of outcomes similar to Meyers et al. (1990), except that her subjects also monitored their understanding. Phillips' (1988) Grade-6 good readers considered alternative interpretations of text, confirmed previous interpretations of text during subsequent reading, monitored when emerging interpretations conflicted with prior knowledge or previous interpretations, shifted focus when reading, and empathized with character perspectives in a story. Of course, this is only a very small set of the many processes covered in chapter 3. In contrast, in the most complete of the reports of experts reading in their domains (e.g., Lundeberg, 1987; Wyatt et al., 1993), there is evidence of use of strategies, monitoring, and evaluation, with active reading occurring from overview to postreading reflection. That is, in the most complete reports of experts reading in their areas of expertise, all of the major categories of constructive responsivity reviewed in chapter 3 are represented. (For example, if Lundeberg's, 1987, or Wyatt et al.'s, 1993, data were to be rescored in terms of the scoring schemes applied by Meyers et al., 1990, and Kucan, 1993, to their child data, the adults would be rated as carrying out all of the major categories of processes in those schemes.)

How did domain experts become so constructively responsive in their reading? Bereiter and Scardamalia (1993) offered an analysis of the development of expertise that we believe might be telling with respect to the development of constructively responsive reading. They contend that experts become good by putting themselves in demanding situations and solving demanding problems. Thus, in the case of reading, a way to become a good reader should be to tackle demanding texts often, texts that require considerable constructive responsivity in order to understand them. Why were the social scientists in Wyatt et al. (1993), the physicists in Bazerman (1985), the law professors in Lundeberg (1987), and the historians in Wineberg (1991) so constructively responsive? According to Bereiter and Scardamalia (1993), it is because they have spent much of their careers reading texts that require constructive responsivity in order to understand them—such as journal articles, legal briefs and cases, and original historical documents. Of course, Bereiter and Scardamalia's (1993) conclusion about the development of expertise through experience in realistic problem solving is consistent with the general constructivist conviction that in order to learn how to do complex things at a high level of proficiency, what is necessary is extensive practice doing complex things (see Driscoll, 1994, chapter 11). From this perspective, constructively responsive reading cannot be taught through drill and practice of the strategies, monitoring, and evaluative processes that comprise constructive responses or through practice applying strategies, monitoring processes, and evaluative analyses to simple texts. Great composers have become good through repeated composing; famous artists honed their talents by creating art; great chess players mastered their game by playing it; and expert radiologists have been reading radiograms for years!!

Can contemporary reading educators produce more certainly constructively evaluative reading than educators have in the past? The current emphasis on students reading authentic texts is certainly a valid approach to teaching reading in light of Bereiter and Scardamalia's (1993) belief that authentic experiences are more likely to lead to expertise than inauthentic ones. An important point made by Bereiter and Scardamalia is that experts keep pushing themselves to the edge of their competence and thus, a curriculum in which students are encouraged to read materials that increase in difficulty as reader competence increases makes sense. On that score, we are not so certain that students are really being pushed to read the most demanding and realistic texts they might be able to handle, ones requiring extensive construction in order to feel confident that the main points have been extracted. More optimistically, we are encouraged that with every passing year we see more and more programs encouraging students to read really demanding materials. For example, students may be asked to conduct collaborative research projects that integrate reading from different knowledge domains, such as social studies and science. We also acknowledge that having students develop into constructively responsive readers is not simply a matter of text selection: constructive responsivity grows as developing readers gain experience and motivation from different purposes for reading, undertaken with motivation from working toward goals others may demand, or those set by readers themselves.

When we examine the processes summarized in chapter 3 as comprising constructively responsive reading, we are struck that many of the processes are now taught to students as part of the reform of comprehension instruction that has been in progress since the 1980s (e.g., Pearson & Fielding, 1991). Based in part on findings from basic research establishing the benefits of teaching specific comprehension processes (e.g., see Pressley, Johnson, Symons, McGoldrick, & Kurita, 1989), elementary-level students are being taught to overview text before attempting to read it, predict the content of text based on information obtained during overviewing, check predictions, make notes, self-question, seek clarification when confused, visualize the meaning of text, check understanding through self-testing, and summarize text. Such teaching definitely makes a difference in the short term, with increasing evidence that instruction of a repertoire of such strategies can increase strategic processing of reading in the long term (e.g., Brown & Pressley, 1994; Rosenshine & Meister, 1992).

A particularly optimistic observation is that some reading educators are teaching in a way that stimulates constructively responsive reading as we described it in chapter 3 (e.g., Gaskins & Elliot, 1991; Pressley, El-Dinary, Gaskins et al., 1992). In these schools, students are taught manageable repertoires of reading strategies, such as the ones listed in the last paragraph. They are taught to monitor their comprehension as they read. Moreover, students are encouraged to use the strategies they are learning to come to evaluative, personally interpretive perspectives on what they read.

Students in these settings are taught such strategies in a constructivist fashion (Harris & Pressley, 1991; Moshman, 1982; Pressley, Harris, & Marks, 1992). Teachers explain and model use of strategies, but this is only the beginning of student acquisition of the strategies. Teachers scaffold student practice and application to the strategic procedures, providing support, re-explanations, and additional modeling as needed. The child does not learn a rigidly prescribed set of procedures, but rather experiences strategies as procedures that can be stretched and adapted depending on task characteristics and demands. With opportunities to apply strategic knowledge across the school day, there is plenty of opportunity to practice diverse application of strategies and to observe the teacher and peers use strategies creatively. Strategies in these classrooms are used in the service of accomplishing whole tasks, such as understanding whole readings, with the comprehension of a reading always the focus of instruction. Reading strategies are presented as tools for making meaning and developing personal interpretations (e.g., personalized visualizations of story actions, summaries emphasizing aspects of a reading considered significant by the reader). Use of strategies is not in pursuit of a correct meaning, but as part of personal understanding and interpretation, with recognition that different readers will find different meanings in readings. Indeed, there is a great deal of interpretive discussion in classrooms where strategies are taught well, with the message clear that strategies can be used in a variety of ways, depending on one's personal proclivities and the characteristics of the text. Varied uses of reading are modeled by teachers, with reading instruction embedded in different curricular and social contexts. Such classrooms emphasize that the meaning of text will differ from student to student largely because what students bring to text differs, with students encouraged to use strategies to relate their background knowledge to what they read (e.g., an important strategy in effective strategy instruction classrooms is simply to relate points made in text to prior knowledge).

Such instruction contrasts with instruction that involves teaching students to execute a fixed sequence of processes as they go through text (e.g., prediction, questioning, seeking clarification, and summarization, as occurs during reciprocal teaching; Palincsar & Brown, 1984). There is nothing fixed about constructively responsive reading, with excellent readers flexibly, opportunistically, and appropriately using the many procedures that comprise skilled reading (i.e., the rich repertoire of processes summarized in chapter 3). To the extent that the framework developed in this volume is credible, it is a mistake to teach children to execute reading processes in a particular order.

Whether the more flexible instruction we favor really leads to the full-blown constructively responsive reading documented in chapter 3 is impossible to say at this time. However, we cannot help but believe that long-term exposure to and encouragement of the subprocesses that constitute constructively responsive reading must increase their use somewhat. The theory underlying such instruction is that learning of all types of information is encouraged by such instruction, for strategic reading should result in more being learned from every encounter with text. If that is so, readers who learn to use strategies should increasingly be in a better position to make informed evaluations about the content of new readings. That is, applying strategies to science reading will increase immediate comprehension and long-term retention of what has been read, with the long-term knowledge gained then available to assist in understanding and evaluating new science texts (e.g., when a student remembers what he or she read about monarch butterflies migrating to Mexico and can relate it to a later science reading on seasonal migration in general).

The exceptionally capable strategy instruction just described is also notable because it is offered in the long term. Thus, even those who are optimistic that constructively responsive reading can be taught recognize that reading involving articulation of strategies, monitoring processes, and evaluative analyses is a long-term development. We are struck that we know of no credible analysis that would suggest that constructively responsive reading could ever be developed quickly, or neatly packaged. The only certainty at this point is that at least some readers who become deeply invested in challenging reading and do a great deal of it seem to develop into constructively responsive readers—such as the lawyers and scholars who were clearly constructively responsive in some of the protocol analyses summarized in chapter 3. It is not known at this point in time whether constructively responsive reading will develop as a function of long-term educational efforts encouraging the use of reading strategies, the monitoring of comprehension, and the use of prior knowledge to understand and evaluate text.[1] Determining whether it does is important, for there are both pragmatic and theoretical implications if such teaching proves effective. At a minimum, there would be clear support for providing education that can contribute to the development of constructively responsive reading.

It is clear that expert readers have considerable experience reading varied texts for varied purposes. These experiences provide a wealth of knowledge related to the social contexts of reading. We consider student familiarity with the range of social contexts and purposes for reading as a final requirement for instruction and experiences that encourage student development as constructively responsive readers. The context in which expert readers read is one that often combines facility in strategy use and response to text with motivation. The social context gives meaning to the reader's meaning construction, for example, as when Wyatt et al.'s (1993) social scientists clearly worked very hard to understand the meanings in articles relating to academic problems that were important to them.

SUMMARY

A number of models of text processing have been proposed and considered prominently in recent research. All are inspired by particular views of predominant processes in comprehension. When the results of the protocol analyses are concatenated, as they were in chapter 3, it is clear that all of the processes favored in these various theories—strategic, metacognitive, knowledge-based, and social—in fact are part of skilled reading. None of the formal models in the literature, however, capture well the diverse processes represented in the chapter 3 summary. The closest to doing so with respect to breadth is reader response theory, although this perspective is very vague with respect to particular operations (i.e., specific strategies, particular ways knowledge affects comprehension processes).

Our response to this situation is to propose a new theory. The concatenation process leading up to chapter 3 was a type of qualitative theoretical analysis as prescribed by Strauss and Corbin (1990). Essentially, we dimensionalized the various comprehension processes observed in the protocol analysis studies—that

---

[1]Right now, the longest-term evaluation of such teaching has been 1 year, with clear differences in the constructive responsivity of second-grade children between those who received a year of such instruction and those who received very good, conventional reading instruction (Brown & Pressley, 1994).

is, we sorted the data in pursuit of an orderly representation of the processes represented in the protocols. There are enough studies completed at this point, and they vary so greatly in their specific characteristics, that most of the processes that constitute conscious reading are now represented in the literature and thus, now summarized in chapter 3. In Strauss and Corbin's (1990) terminology, the model is close to being saturated in that new think-aloud studies are not resulting in dramatic improvements in the chapter 3 classification scheme.

We characterize reading according to our new model as constructively responsive, capturing the reader constructions that are so essential to meaning construction but emphasizing that those constructions are in response to the particular text being processed. We note that Rosenblatt (1938) in her earliest writing on reader response theory similarly emphasized what we would call reader constructivity (i.e., active processing of text that is greatly affected by highly personal prior knowledge), constructivity that was respectful of the text. We note as well that even radical literary critics who once advanced positions emphasizing the constructive aspects of reading over fixed meaning in a text are now coming to the position that compelling responses to text are limited by information in the text and that good interpretations account for many of the points made in a text (e.g., Eco, 1990). We feel that there is theoretical triangulation going on here (Mathison, 1988), with theorists who initially advanced diverse perspectives on comprehension processes coming to a similar conclusion that both reader constructivity and text characteristics matter in comprehension and thus, strengthening confidence in our conclusion that good reading is constructively responsive. No one could doubt that our long-term commitment to information processing analyses is a very different starting point with respect to text analysis than the literary criticism traditions with which Rosenblatt and Eco identify and yet, in the 1990s, all of us are describing constructive processing that is text responsive.

Constructively responsive reading is expertise in reading from our perspective, and in the third section of this chapter, we made the case that the reading documented in chapter 3 is consistent with other expert performances. In other arenas, a rather strong case can be made that expertise is the result of very long-term learning and development and thus, constructively responsive reading is probably more an appropriate endgoal of one's entire reading education rather than a goal that might be attained in the elementary grades. Still, it is encouraging that elementary-level instruction is being devised that fosters the acquisition of constructively responsive reading. The assessments of this instruction that are now available permit optimism that such teaching really can move young readers closer to the ideal of constructively responsive reading, although not nearly enough assessment has been undertaken to date to permit confidence in this conclusion. Certainly, assessments of students' development as constructively responsive readers need to reflect the diversity of strategies and responses we might expect from the students. Although some young students are making good progress toward being constructively responsive (Holdaway, 1979), familiarizing every young student with this type of reading seems like a good idea to us, one that deserves a great deal of research attention. Young readers who draw on their experiences with language, who use their imaginations, who are passionate about reading and being read to, and who have the opportunity to discuss what they read and how they read might be well prepared to become expert in constructively responsive reading. Although we hold full constructive responsivity as a benchmark that is probably reached only through considerable experience in reading, we note that a developmental tack on the theory supports instructional practice and independent reading that includes a variety of texts, tasks, and social settings.

One reaction we received from colleagues who read chapter 3 was that the number of processes reviewed there was overwhelming. We agree and thus offered in Table 4.1 a thumbnail sketch of constructively responsive reading, with the table summarizing the ways readers can respond to a text in general. We believe young readers will benefit from learning to respond to texts in the ways summarized in Table 4.1. Of course, we also believe that much experience attempting to do so as one reads challenging texts is essential before the repertoire of responses in Table 4.1 becomes habitual.

Finally, we end this chapter as we began it, pointing out that constructive responsivity subsumes all of the processes favored in the theories of text processing proposed previously:

1. Reader responding as conceived by Rosenblatt (1938, 1978) is central to constructive responsivity.
2. Constructively responsive readers control their use of strategies through monitoring, as Baker and Brown (1984) described it.
3. The top-down processing summarized by schema theory (e.g., R. C. Anderson & Pearson, 1984) is in constructively responsive reading; so is the bottom-up processing emphasized by van Dijk and Kintsch (1983).
4. Constructively responsive reading is massively inferential. Constructively responsive reading is socially embedded, with construction and responsivity often in the service of social goals.

Constructively responsive reading is very complex, much more complex than presented in previous conceptions of reading. As complex as it is, it is orderly in that readers intelligently articulate strategic processes, monitoring, and knowledge of the world.

If we ended the book at this point, it would be a happy ending. The protocol analyses of skilled reading permit a new theory, one that is more comprehensive than previous theoretical efforts. We are not ending on that note, however, for our time spent with the various protocol analyses also permits insights about this methodology that we believe need to be aired. As great as the contributions of protocol analyses to understanding consciously skilled reading have been, we believe the potential is much greater. Indeed, our view is that the way the methodology has been used to date has minimized the insights that might be gained from the approach. Thus, the next chapter, which does conclude the volume, reflects additionally on the state of protocol analyses of skilled reading today and directions that we believe, if pursued, would permit much more to be learned about reading.

5
▼▼▼▼▼▼▼

The Future of Reading Protocol Analyses: Addressing Methodological Concerns in Order to Advance Conceptual Understanding

In closing a book in which we have made so much of verbal reports, it might seem natural that we would provide high praise for the studies to date and the methods used in the studies. However, the more time we spent with this literature, the more convinced we were that these verbal report studies might better serve as markers on a path that can lead to more sophisticated and ambitious, and certainly more methodologically rigorous and detailed, studies. We are convinced that verbal self-reporting remains an underdeveloped methodology. Rather than place these concerns up front in this volume and thus, seem to undermine our conceptual efforts based on the self-report data generated to date, we elected to close the volume with commentary on methodology, using these concerns to suggest important research directions for the future, ones that can advance a conceptual understanding of both reading and protocol analysis as a valuable means of investigating reading.

We should emphasize that we think that the methods used to date were good enough to permit high confidence in the conclusions that we offered earlier in this volume. In chapter 3, we identified conscious processes that people can use in their reading, processes revealed through protocol analyses. We believe that much greater understanding of reading is possible, however, with additional insights in understanding reading through protocol analyses dependent on improvement of methods used in protocol studies.

The numerous and diverse methodological issues related to verbal reports made it difficult to construct a seamless discussion of the methodology and the future of protocol analysis. Thus, we are aware that this chapter may seem less coherently tied than the previous chapters in this volume: a series of related concerns but ones not always strongly connected. We did not want to imply that the issues in this chapter are more tightly knit than they are. Thus, there are no unnatural bridges in this concluding chapter or transitions suggesting more relationship between issues than exist.

This chapter is also something of an advertisement for the utility of the exercise summarized in the earlier chapters of this book. We make the case in what follows that exhaustive knowledge of the potential conscious processes involved in reading—and we believe that is what chapter 3 reflects—permits some analytical possibilities that were not possible before the chapter 3 analysis.

We begin this chapter with the most striking problem with respect to methodology. We confronted this problem every time we sat down with the literature reviewed in this book, one that must be addressed and solved.

SPECIFICITY (COMPLETENESS) OF THE DESCRIPTIONS OF METHODS IN READING PROTOCOL ANALYSES

The greatest challenge facing us was to deal with the lack of specificity in many of the studies we reviewed. The methods were greatly underspecified in many studies, often in ways that either decreased our certainties about the researchers' interpretations or made it impossible for us to come to interpretations of our own with confidence. Rather than point out the concerns in particular studies, we offer here a summary of what we believe are the minimum points that should be covered in any methods section. There were a number of studies that, with sufficient attention to the features we address in this section, might have yielded even more useful information about skilled reading.

First, it is essential that the *characteristics of the subjects* (i.e., the readers in a study) be detailed. It is particularly critical to know the reading abilities of the participants. Yes, we know of the debates about such measurement and that standardized measurement is out of the question with respect to extremely expert readers (e.g., professionals with many years of experience in their discipline). Still, providing whatever information possible, related to subjects' reading ability, is helpful. Many studies consider graduate student, professor, or professional status to be a proxy for expert reader status. We are certain that this convenient practice masks considerable individual differences in how these readers construct understanding and respond to text.

Subjects come to verbal report studies with diverse experiences and knowledge. We believe that verbal report researchers should check and disclose subjects' familiarity with the verbal reporting methodology, and subjects' familiarity with the task to be reported on. For example, we anticipate that a student pursuing a doctoral degree in literary theory, who minored in American Civil War history as an undergraduate and who has participated previously in verbal reporting studies, will read and give verbal reports about the short story "Occurrence at

Owl Creek Bridge" in a manner quite different from a student who has no familiarity with verbal reports, literary theory, Ambrose Bierce, or the American Civil War. Attention to such matters of subject characteristics may help both researchers and readers of research to interpret verbal report data. Also, it is important to note the degree that subjects' personalities may have affected the verbal reporting (e.g., How does the subject interact with the examiner? Does the subject appear comfortable with the task of verbal reporting, and making public personal reactions, insights, and interpretations?).

A related issue is the *characteristics of the texts*, and in particular, relative to the characteristics of the readers. Although we recognize the impossibility and the inappropriateness of specifying the grade level of the text(s) read in many protocol investigations (e.g., when domain experts read journal articles in their fields), it is not too much to ask that as full discussion as possible of the texts be provided. Sometimes the most reasonable way to describe the texts is to reproduce them in an appendix. By doing so, future reviewers of the research can evaluate the texts using whatever criteria they would prefer or consider appropriate. It is also appropriate to describe the physical quality of the text. For example, if text is presented on a computer screen in a sentence-by-sentence manner (as compared with a text on paper that can be flipped or turned, where rereading, skimming, searching, and reacting is made easier), constructive responsivity might be influenced.

We were particularly struck that the *directions* given to subjects were frequently not provided or specified very vaguely. The directions provided to subjects can color their self-reports, a point understood since Ericsson and Simon's (1984/1993) detailed review. Thus, it is critical that the directions given to participants be available for review and analysis. We recommend as much verbatim presentation as possible of the directions in methods sections, although we recognize this is challenging because there is a frequent need in protocol analyses to rephrase and re-explain thinking-aloud directions. In addition, an account of any reminders given to subjects as they read and think aloud would be helpful.

As part of the directions, most studies included practice in generating think-alouds in reaction to text. The directions and nature of such practice were almost always presented vaguely, again probably because there was some necessary variability in directions and practice depending on subject understanding of directions and task requirements. It is essential that every effort be made to portray exactly how participating readers were informed about what they were to do, even if that is only to provide an indication of the range of re-explanations that were used by the experimenter in reaction to participant difficulties. Did the subjects receive feedback in practice sessions? Were subjects coached? Because many of the studies that we examined involved only about 10 minutes or so of practice, the amount of practice that needs to be documented in reporting on the nature of think-aloud studies is not overwhelming.

We note as well that there were few reports on formal checks of reader understanding of directions, although our impression was that many researchers simply kept the practice going until the readers seemed to be doing what the researcher expected. Formal checks and formal reporting of whatever checks occurred (even informal ones) would make think-aloud studies much easier to interpret, for there would be increased certainty in the minds of the readers studying the reports that the subjects actually acted as they were asked to act. There were few accounts of the nature of interactions between subjects and experimenters during the reading of the text. For example, the disclosure that an examiner intervened in the reading of a text is important to know, but it is important also to include information about when the intervention occurred, how the experimenter determined that the intervention was necessary, and what exactly was said or done during the intervention.

The *methods of analyses* were also incompletely reported. Coding of verbal reports is an interpretive act, and the richness of language and the constructive nature of understanding language represent the promise and challenge of using verbal reports to describe constructive responsivity. It is imperative that researchers provide full accounts of the means used to develop categories and to code reports. This includes a description of the relevant research, theory, experimenter hunches, and their meeting points (i.e., categories used). The degree to which previous theoretical, empirical, and descriptive work helps frame verbal report data will provide an opportunity to examine how verbal report data contribute to the evolution of thought and understanding about reading matters.

At a minimum, there needs to be clear description of *categories used to score think-alouds*, with these perhaps best explained through the use of illustrations. The studies varied tremendously in the number and detail of examples provided. Our view is that the more examples from actual reader protocols, the better. One strong suspicion is that we were often looking at best examples in the reports we read, perhaps because many of the verbalizations really were not that obviously classifiable! One possibility is that the expansive set of categories detailed in chapter 3 will permit many more protocol responses to be easily categorized (more about this point later in the chapter). If so, this will permit much more extensive provision of examples that we believe would be so helpful in advancing understanding of reader processing by consumers of protocol analyses research.

Although many reports of *reliability* were included in the studies we reviewed, there were some studies in which there was no hint of a reliability check. Attention to interrater reliability in coding readers' actions is imperative. One possibility is that high reliabilities were not obtained in some of these investigations. Again, the provision of the detailed set of categories in chapter 3 may contribute to improving the situation, if that was a problem. Another possibility is to score strategies in as fine-grained a fashion as possible, but then only report classifications at a level of specificity that is reliable. Thus, Meyers et al. (1990) reported that there was reasonably high reliability in classifying responses with respect to the six main analysis categories in their study and much lower reliability for more fine-grained classifications within the larger categories. Thus, their published report emphasized the six-category scheme. If it is questionable whether individual instances of processes can be counted reliably, one tactic is not to report exact numbers of occurrences of particular processes, but categories of frequencies of occurrence such as "never," "a few occurrences of the process," and "many observations of the process." Even if raters cannot agree whether a response occurred two or four times, often they can agree that it occurred a few times. Moreover, whether a response occurred 10 or 20 times is usually not as critical as concluding that it occurred many times compared to other responses that occurred only a few times or never (see Olshavsky, 1976–1977; Shearer et al., 1993; Wyatt et al., 1993). In any case, we do not believe a study intended to suggest generalizable findings should be published if the scoring is not provably reliable.

An additional concern is how verbal report excerpts are chosen for inclusion in research reports as illustrations. We suspect that most excerpts included in write-ups show the researcher's strong hand. True, a rich example of a reader constructively responding to text can have great explanatory power. But are all examples coded as compelling as the ones presented as examples? Do they in fact represent the thinking activity that the researcher would like to generalize from the excerpt provided? We believe that a detailed account of how examples are chosen, and information about the representativeness of examples would further clarify verbal report data and enhance their value.

We also believe that the fullest possible accounting of the theories that were used in framing a verbal report study will help consumers of the research best understand reports of think-aloud studies. For example, a study examining reader response or evaluative processes in literary criticism might focus on evaluative remarks made by a subject, or the intertextuality of a reader's comments. A cognitive psychologist might interpret the same transcripts of verbal reports (or the examples contained in a book or journal article) from a perspective that emphasizes strategy use. Although this is not an unhealthy situation, the researcher's ability to describe where coding and categorization schemes derive from is at least helpful. One person's noise may be another's critical result.

In short, the studies reviewed in preparation of this volume were often challenging in that they contained much less information than should be expected from scientific reports. We suspect that some of the vagueness in reporting reflected fuzziness in methods. That is, in providing practice until readers were thinking aloud as the researcher wanted, feedback and additional instruction was probably offered in an ad hoc fashion. Similarly, scoring criteria may have been created along the way in many studies, which is not so bad so long as ultimately it is possible to provide some principles for the scoring and some assurance that the data actually fit the ultimate categories as described (more about the development of scoring schemes later in this chapter). Our view is that protocol researchers need to give some very hard thought to how they can make their reports as complete as possible. We suspect and hope that the distinctions offered in this volume, especially the chapter 3 categorizations of potentially conscious processes in reading, will contribute to improving the situation. Attention to the detail of the methodology of protocol analyses cannot help but reduce skepticism about the veridicality of verbal reports with the thought processes they are intended to reflect, a topic that receives additional attention in the next section.

BELIEVABILITY (VALIDITY) OF SELF-REPORTS

Without a doubt, the greatest concern about self-reports from the research community in general is whether they are believable. Do they really reflect the cognitive processes that are being reported? One obvious tactic in validating such self-reports is to attempt to relate them to objective performance. Thus, readers who are more constructively active might be expected to understand and recall text better (or at least differently) than readers who are not so active (Ericsson & Simon, 1984/1993). Also, reading speed, efficiency, or other performance indicators (e.g., eye movements) might be expected to vary with use of reported strategies (Afflerbach & Johnston, 1984).

Somewhat surprisingly, protocol analysts have done relatively little of this type of validation; for example, relatively little examination of relationships between self-reported processing and comprehension and/or other indicators of processing. Much more positively, however, when researchers have attempted to validate self-reports in this fashion, the self-reports have proven credible.

What are some positive pieces of evidence? Meyers et al. (1990) obtained a correlation between measures of their fourth- and fifth-grade students' comprehension and their self-reported reasoning and claims of understanding. Guthrie et al. (1991) reported that the strategies self-reported by college students as they searched documents for information correlated with their search efficiency. Olson et al. (1981) observed correlations between self-reported strategies at particular points in text and the speed of processing at those points. For example, reading was slower early in a story when readers reported storing background information presented in the story and formulating hypotheses about the stories read. At points where substantial inferential activities were reported, processing was slower. Subjects reported simply confirming their suspicions as they finished text with relatively rapid reading times near the end of text. In Trabasso and Suh (1993), self-reported inferential activities predicted a variety of performance measures related to the inferences, including reading times and long-term retention of stories.

In addition, there is not much evidence to suggest a lack of relationship between self-reports and performance outcomes. Some believe the most damaging piece of data was generated by Wade et al. (1990). Wade and her colleagues examined the overall patterns of strategy use reports by the college students in their studies, producing six types of profiles of text processing, varying from ones that reflected extensive constructive responding to text to superficial constructive responding. These classifications were not associated with significant differences in immediate memory for text, however. In weighing this piece of evidence, we believe a very strong trend in the data should be considered.

By far, one of Wade et al.'s groups was more sophisticated in their strategies use than any of the other five. This group, which Wade et al. (1990) referred to as "good strategy users," following a categorization suggested by Pressley et al. (1987), were more diverse in their constructive responses to text than other participants in the study. Good strategy users made notes, paraphrased, outlined, and/or constructed diagrams as they read. They varied their reading speed from skimming to slowing, and they reread when it was necessary. They made use of their notes and mental notings to review the text read after reading. With respect to recall, there was a strong trend in the data favoring the good strategy users, with more than one half standard deviation recall difference relative to the next best group with respect to recall of important information in the text. Good strategy users also recalled descriptively more unimportant information than other members of the sample, although their recall advantage for unimportant information was not as striking as for important information. Because there were very few subjects in the good strategy user classification in Wade et al.'s (1990) study (i.e., six), there was low statistical power for detecting anything but smashing effects in comparisons of good strategy user recall with other recall levels in the study. Thus, our view is that although Wade et al. (1990) is considered by some as failing to provide validation for reading strategy self-reports, there is little reason to be confident in the conclusion that the validation failed. In fact, there was a pretty striking trend favoring the recall of the subjects who were the most strategic.

Despite the fact that there is more good news than bad news with respect to validation, there really is not enough validation data, especially given the potential conclusions that might be drawn from verbal protocols of reading. For example, in the last chapter we argued in favor of constructive responsivity theory as more inclusive than all previous theories of text processing, which is a very strong claim—much too strong if there are serious doubts about the validity of verbal self-reports during reading! From our perspective, there is a great need for much more validation of verbal protocols.

Verbal reports often require considerable inferences for a researcher describing reading behavior. Typically, the researcher analyzing verbal reports is operating from a knowledge base that includes a construct or series of constructs, such as reading comprehension or response to literature. These constructs inform the identification and coding of verbal report transcripts. A critical aspect of the coding process in construction of meaning from verbal report transcripts is the language used by each participant in the study. People vary considerably in their manner of communication and the words and phrases used to characterize their own thoughts, strategies, reactions, and interactions with text. Given this potential variation in subjects' reporting, the inferences made based on verbal reports may benefit from multiple indicators of the nature of the reader's interaction with text. Triangulation of measures can provide a degree of confidence that the chain of inference from eliciting, recording, transcribing, analyzing, categorizing, and reporting on verbal reports is defensible.

We are encouraged that several researchers of text processing are giving some hard thought to potential ways of triangulating verbal report data and strengthening confidence in conclusions that might be drawn from think-aloud reports. For example, Magliano and Graesser (1993) recommended a three-pronged approach for drawing conclusions about text processing. One prong is conducting a theoretical analysis of the processing that might be expected in the particular situation. The second prong is verbal protocol analysis. The third is collection of behavioral measures, such as objective memory of text, reading times, and so on. The goal is for all three prongs to be aligned. The closer and more consistent the alignment of verbal report data with what is anticipated a priori, and with the product measures generated from the investigation, the higher the level of confidence one can have in each.

Magliano and Graesser's (1993) approach goes beyond previous validation efforts, which have involved correlating verbal process reports with other measurements, by increasing the prominence of theory in the validation process. Without a theory, all one will have is a lot of data. Thus, we believe one strength of the work reported in this volume is that we did come to a theory encompassing the mass of verbal protocol data that now exist. The weakest of the three prongs with respect to the existing reading protocol database is with respect to demonstrated correlations between objective measures of text processing and verbal reports that are expected based on theory. As validation efforts proceed, we urge careful attention to the establishment of clear linkages between theory, verbal process reports, and other measures that can be complementary to verbal self-reports. We believe this work will do much to bring verbal reports from the status of a "bootstrap operation" (Ericsson & Simon, 1984/1993) to a maturing methodology.

This work is important not only for the establishment of the validity of verbal process reports, but also for increasing confidence in the validity of other measures, such as recall and reading time. Although reading researchers have traditionally relied on the latter measures as indirect indicators of process, confidence in their validity will be increased to the extent that arguably more direct indicators of process, such as verbal process reports, provide convergent support for the conclusions emanating from analyses of recall and reading time data. Thus, many cognitive psychologists have been willing to put more faith in nonvalidated recall and reading time data than in nonvalidated protocol reports; in truth, "objective" data and self-report data can go far in validating one another.

As we argue for increased validation of verbal self-reports, it is not to imply that any study not correlating verbal self-reports with other measures of outcome should be dismissed. Rather, as it becomes clearer that verbal self-reports do link with processing reliably, confidence should increase in conclusions from studies in which only the verbal self-reports are collected. This is important for there are some occasions when quantitative correlations between verbal self-reports and other measures would be difficult; for example, when readers each read pieces of their own selection (see Wyatt et al., 1993). It is also important because the collection of verbal self-reports alone is expensive and cumbersome. Adding the requirement that other measures must also be collected, especially if it has already been established that verbal process reports are associated with such measures, increases the expense and, ultimately, will decrease the number of protocol analyses that will be conducted. As should be clear already in this chapter, we believe that further investigations using protocol analyses will be beneficial, so that there is high incentive for finding ways to do them economically.

ADHERENCE TO THE METHODOLOGICAL STRICTURES RECOMMENDED BY ERICSSON AND SIMON (1984/1993)

get this!

An important question to address is just how closely the verbal reports in the reading studies are consistent with Ericsson and Simon's (1984/1993) prescriptions for such reports, which is critical given the high regard for the Ericsson and Simon volume among cognitive scientists in general, and the high percentage of verbal report studies that cite their work, whether the focus of the study is cognitive process or reader response. In fact, we noted tremendous variability in adherence to the Ericsson and Simon (1984/1993) guidelines as we read the studies reviewed for preparation of this book. In drawing this conclusion, we add that we believe that, in some cases, there was good reason to depart from the Ericsson and Simon guidelines or at least reason to consider doing so. Unfortunately, the reading self-report studies have not been analytical enough to permit confident conclusions about whether Ericsson and Simon's (1984/1993) guidelines should be strictly adhered to in studying text processing. In fact, the greater the discrepancy between the "fuzzy" and multidimensional tasks readers are asked to undertake and report on, and the "pure" types of problem-solving that drew the attention of earlier protocol analysts, the more critical it is to examine guidelines for reporting. We consider here three particular methodological issues raised by Ericsson and Simon (1984/1993).

Concurrent or Retrospective Processing

Recall from chapter 1 that Ericsson and Simon (1984/1993) claimed that verbal reports are most believable to the extent that they reflect the current contents of short-term memory, and that they are reports of current processing. Was that the case in the reading studies? Did subjects concurrently report the content of their thoughts as they read? In some cases, the answer appears to be yes. For example, in Bereiter and Bird (1985), subjects read text aloud and were asked to express their thoughts the moment they came to mind. Earthman (1989, 1992) used a similar procedure, as did Rogers (1991), Schmalhofer and Boschert (1988), Trabasso and Suh (1993), and Wyatt et al. (1993). Charney (1993) directed her participants to say whatever thoughts came into their heads while they read. She explained this process to her subjects by indicating that many people mumble thoughts to themselves while they read and thus, their task in the study was to raise the volume of these mumblings.

More commonly, however, subjects were asked to provide retrospective reports, ones that were separated somewhat in time from the actual reading. Ericsson and Simon (1984/1993) made the case that the closer in time such retrospective reports were to when the actual processing occurred, the more likely that traces of the processing that occurred (e.g., during reading) would remain in short-term memory and thus be reportable. Although, in general, the retrospective reports in the reading studies occurred close in time to when the actual reading occurred, it is impossible to assess from these studies whether the reports reflected traces remaining in short-term memory or were reconstructions by subjects of what happened as they read. This is a problem because such reconstructions might reflect more the readers' theories of reading than the actual processing they engaged in.

Olshavsky's (1976–1977) study did much to influence the use of retrospective reporting in think-aloud studies of reading. Yellow dots occurred at various points in the readings in her study, with subjects directed to verbalize when they encountered the dots. Since that study, there have been many studies in which dots (or their equivalents) are placed in readings with readers directed to self-verbalize about their reading processes at the sign of the dot (e.g., Afflerbach, 1990b; Lytle, 1982; Pritchard, 1990a; Wood & Zakaluk, 1992). However, because these studies presented readings of different length and different numbers of dots, and because some subjects were encouraged to report at any time (cf. Afflerbach, 1990b), the length of time and amount of text between self-reports varied between studies. In no case, however, were dots presented as frequently as every sentence, so that each reader self-report reflected processing that occurred at least over several sentences.

In other studies, participants have been asked to self-verbalize after processing a particular amount of text. The smaller the amount of text read for each report, the more certain it would seem that the report would reflect the contents of short-term memory accurately. Thus, it is noteworthy that some studies had subjects stop after every sentence and self-report, such as Fletcher (1986) and Olson et al. (1981). In other studies, however, the unit of text read was longer (e.g., Phillips, 1988; Wade et al., 1990). Sometimes subjects have been instructed to verbalize after reading the text, with the subjects themselves permitted to decide when they will self-report (e.g., Graves & Frederiksen, 1991). We note that the manner in which text is presented to the reader can influence the nature of the reporting. For example, Olson et al. (1981) had subjects read texts in a sentence-by-sentence manner as single sentences were presented on a computer screen. Here the control of the amount of text may yield more reports that have considerable basis in short-term memory.

Does it make a difference whether the verbal reports are concurrent or retrospective? How much of a difference is made, if any at all? Unfortunately, these are impossible questions to answer, for there has been little systematic study of the consequences of concurrent versus delayed reporting on the conclusions about processing that are made based on the self-reports. In addition, the nature of reporting (in terms of concurrency or retrospectivity) may be influenced by differential training, coaching, or prompting that subjects receive. We noted earlier that there has been little systematic accounting of the specifics of examiner prompting of subjects, or the nature of training that subjects receive for giving verbal reports. If this information were included, it would further help our understanding of where verbal reports come from. That is, it was often difficult to determine the concurrency of the reports summarized in studies we reviewed in preparing this book.

Ericsson and Simon (1984/1993, chap. 5) reported a few relevant comparisons of concurrent and retrospective processing and concluded that there were few differences between concurrent reports and ones collected after a few sentences had been read. Our informal examination of the concurrent and retrospective reports suggests that Ericsson and Simon's conclusion is probably correct, with both concurrent and retrospective reports varying greatly in the number of processes documented. Even so, we believe that the concurrency of self-reports is important, because the concurrent and delayed report studies varied in so many other ways (e.g., passages read, directions given to subjects, subject characteristics).

The traditional concerns (see Afflerbach & Johnston, 1984) about concurrency and delay undoubtedly are going to persist in the absence of compelling data informing those concerns. The more delayed the reports, the greater the need to reconstruct what must have been happening rather than simply report what just happened. The more delayed the reports, the more they can be influenced by knowledge gained about text content as reading proceeds. The concern with concurrent reports is that they interfere with online reading and thus, distort natural reading processes. Of course, the same concern can be leveled at delayed reports (see Afflerbach & Johnston, 1984)—for example, that stopping to report after every sentence or every few sentences will shift the nature of subsequent reading.

What is needed is systematic study of these issues, not continued conjecturing about them. The compilation of processes summarized in chapter 3 provides the most complete summary of conscious text processes assembled to date. One important issue is whether concurrent and delayed self-reports are equally sensitive to all of the processes covered in chapter 3. If future concurrent and delayed self-reports of reading are scored for the presence and absence of all these categories, some subtleties (or even not-so-subtle distinctions) between concurrent and delayed reports not apparent in earlier analyses might emerge. The field is in a better position than ever to evaluate the possibility of differences in processing and reporting of processing as a function of concurrency of reporting due to the chapter 3 summary of just what conscious processes can occur during reading.

As we close this subsection, we note one important reason to expect that there might not be much difference between concurrent reports of reading processes and briefly delayed ones. Concurrent reports have been observed to involve reporting of reading that is just completed (Afflerbach & Johnston, 1984; Johnston & Afflerbach, 1985). That is, it may simply be impossible to report what one is doing with respect to what is being read right at this instance. If that is so, there should be very little difference between what researchers claim are concurrent and what they view as briefly retrospective reports. An important question then would be to determine how long reports can be delayed before they are altered by delay. One reason this is a critical issue is that as reports are delayed longer, fewer pauses are required in reading to make such reports and, presumably, reading becomes more natural (i.e., there is less interference with it). Much more needs to be known about the timing of self-reports and the effects of timing differences as part of expanding the science of reading protocol analysis. This examination may in turn contribute to our understanding of protocol analyses across domains of inquiry, as it addresses the issue of differences between thinking aloud and introspection.

Reports of the Content of Short-Term Memory or Interpretations of That Content?

Ericsson and Simon (1984/1993) were clear in their specification that self-reports are better to the extent they reflect the contents of short-term memory rather than the thinker's interpretation of the processes or description of them. Thus, if a subject in a list-memory study reports, "Put the dog, cat, cow, and alligator in one pile," and "I'm moving the apple, orange, tomato, and grape into another pile," and finally, "that leaves a pile with a truck, car, and bulldozer in it," it is a better verbalization than if the subject remarks, "I'm using categorization as a strategy to learn this list." The researcher can be much more certain of categorizing processes in the former case than in the latter case, at least as far as Ericsson and Simon are concerned.

Given this stricture, it is perhaps surprising that some researchers in the studies of conscious processes during reading asked subjects to report on the processes they were using. For example, Afflerbach (1990a) did so, as did Johnston and Afflerbach (1985). Afflerbach (1990b) requested that subjects report the strategies they were using. Wade et al. (1990) asked their subjects to describe any study methods they used while reading. On the other hand, requesting reports of particular strategies gives the researcher a degree of control in restricting the universe of subjects' possible verbalizations, while working with subjects who are knowledgeable about the strategies and responses under investigation may provide focused reports.

One particularly strong piece of advisement offered by Ericsson and Simon (1984/1993) was not to ask subjects to attempt to explain why they were doing what they were doing. Of course, such a direction certainly calls for more than reporting of the contents of short-term memory; it invites theorizing about one's cognitive processes. This subject theorizing should be discouraged, according to the Ericsson and Simon (1984/1993) model. However, Guthrie et al. (1991), for example, asked their subjects to explain why they were doing what they were doing. Schwegler and Shamoon (1991) asked their readers to theorize in another way—to theorize about what the writer was trying to say.

Again, based on the available analyses, it is not really possible to know what difference it makes whether subjects are urged to provide reports of the exact contents of their short-term memories versus reports of their processes by name. It is not really possible to know either what difference it makes that subjects respond to requests to theorize about their reading. We believe that research on these problems is necessary, especially because there are important theoretical implications of being able to report about processes by name and to know why processing is occurring in a particular way. That is, there is more to reading than the cognitive science perspective on problem solving which Ericsson and Simon (1984/1993) favored. From the perspective of metacognitive theory (e.g., Flavell, Miller, & Miller, 1993), subjects who categorize during list learning and know they are categorizing are more cognitively sophisticated than those who categorize but do so with no awareness of the process or its effects on memory. An observation that Pressley and his colleagues have made in their studies of reading strategies instruction is that use of the name of a strategy is a powerful part of teaching students to use the strategic process (e.g., El-Dinary, Pressley, Coy-Ogan, Schuder, & Strategies Instruction Teachers of Burnt Mills Elementary School, 1994). Also, it is clear that metacognitive theory assumes that people who know why they are processing the way they are processing are more competent thinkers than those who lack awareness of why their cognition functions as it does (Flavell et al., 1993). It seems very possible that asking subjects to label their cognitive processes and to explain why they are processing as they are might be very revealing about sophisticated processing.

In particular, it may be especially revealing if unlabeled verbalizations are difficult for the researcher to categorize—if the processes are not really transparent from the verbalizations. In the case of close to automatic processes and ones that are carried out very efficiently, this certainly could be the case. Thus, from a reliability perspective, reader labeling of processes and explanations might increase the dependability of the classification of verbalizations and reduce the need for researcher inference about cognitive processes (see Afflerbach & Johnston, 1984). On the other hand, the closer readers' activities come to automaticity, the more problematic it may be for readers to describe these automatic, or near-automatic happenings.

In summary, we simply do not know what difference it makes whether readers report the actual contents of short-term memory or name the processes they are using and/or explain why they are processing the way that they are. We need to find out if it makes a difference.

Instructions to Elicit Particular Cognitive Behaviors Versus Neutral Instructions

Ericsson and Simon (1984/1993; e.g., chap. 2) argued that think-aloud directions suggesting that there is researcher interest in particular types of processing might very well prompt such processing, a point reiterated by Afflerbach and Johnston (1984). Given this concern, it is notable that reading researchers often did exactly that, with different processes cued in the different studies. The diversity of processes prompted is obvious from these examples: Afflerbach (1990a) told his subjects of the particular interest in prediction, elaboration, and inferencing; Afflerbach (1990b) informed subjects that the study was about main idea construction processes; Fletcher (1986) informed his subjects that their goal should be to be able to create a summary of what they read and thus, possibly informed his subjects about the importance of summarization processes in their think-alouds; Johnston and Afflerbach (1985) also emphasized summarizing in their directions to subjects; Graves and Frederiksen (1991) directed their participants to attend to content and style when reading; Guthrie et al. (1991), who were specifically interested in search processes, asked subjects to report what they were currently looking for; Haas and Flower (1988) emphasized interpretation in their directions to subjects; Phillips (1988) informed her subjects not to restate the text and in fact, required them to make inferences; Pritchard (1990a) named some particular processes as examples of what might be reported in his directions to subjects; Schwegler and Shamoon (1991) prompted their readers toward evaluation of what was being read; and Olson et al. (1981) oriented their subjects toward inferencing, elaborating, drawing connections between sentences, and predicting. It is perhaps telling that in every one of these cases the researchers found evidence for the processes they cued.

In contrast, other researchers have gone to considerable lengths not to suggest processes to their participants, including in the studies reported by Bereiter and Bird (1985), Charney (1993), Earthman (1989, 1992), Lundeberg (1987), Olshavsky (1976–1977), Trabasso and Suh (1993), and Wyatt et al. (1993). All of these studies yield rich reports of readers' interactions with text, including strategy use and response. Given the frequent observation in the social sciences literature that people will often comply with researcher demands, we have to conclude that researcher silence about how the text might be processed is more defensible than directions that prompt particular processes, especially when the goal is to learn about the processes people naturally use when they read. If the question is whether people can use particular processes at all, prompting them to use these processes is sensible. If there is a desire to know what such processes are like when people use them, it is also reasonable to prompt them in order to assure that a sample of the target processes will, in fact, be observed.

The analysis we have just offered should clarify that what is presented in chapter 3 is a summary of the potentially conscious processes in reading. It is not a summary of the ones that naturally occur in the absence of prompting, for as we have made the case here, often the reports that contributed to our analyses involved prompting of particular processes. That such processes occurred in the protocols, even as responses to implicit or explicit directions, establishes only that they are possible as part of conscious reading, not that they will occur frequently or even at all in reading not influenced by experimenter directions or instruction of some type.

Summary

The methodological suggestions made by Ericsson and Simon (1984/1993) reflect their assumptions about the nature of cognitive processing, and some of their methodological claims remain strong, buttressed by both intuitive and empirical support. For example, their contention that researcher instructions can bias processing one way or another is almost beyond dispute. Perhaps less defensible is their reluctance to consider self-reports involving readers classifying or attempting to explain their cognitive processes, especially given metacognitive theoretical claims that such reports can reveal sophistications about thinking that are critical to consider in understanding skilled and not-so-skilled cognition. Unfortunately, however, the protocol analyses have not particularly illuminated critical methodological debates that surround Ericsson and Simon's (1984/1993) prescriptions. We believe such debates should be addressed directly by reading protocol data, and that by doing so more than knowledge of methodology will be affected. Such work has high potential for deepening our understanding of the reading process, a reading process that is recognized now as very complicated.

SENSITIVITY TO SITUATIONAL DETERMINANTS OF CONSTRUCTIVE RESPONSIVITY

People's cognitive responses are situationally determined (Jenkins, 1979). Jenkins argued that human cognitive processes depend on four types of variables in interaction:

1. Subject characteristics: knowledge, short-term memory capacity, spatial ability, age, motivation, and so on.

2. Orienting tasks provided to the subject: instructions, apparatus, reading goal, modality, and so on.

3. Materials being processed: genre, length, difficulty, topic, and so on.

4. Criterion task: free recall, recognition, question answering, summarization, and so on.

Jenkins (1979) depicted these four types of variables as points of a tetrahedron, and thus his perspective that cognitive processing depends on situational variables came to be known as the tetrahedral model. This model has fared well, being consistently cited (e.g., Samuels & Kamil, 1984; van den Broek et al., 1993) when the point is made that cognition is not an all or none affair, but rather the cognition observed depends on situational variables.

In contrast to cognitive psychology in general, which has been sensitive to situational influences and setting effects on cognition (including reading), the reading protocol analysts have been insensitive to situational factors affecting constructive responding to text. A typical design in reading protocol studies involved one type of reader who (a) was provided one type of orienting task; (b) read one, two, or several pieces that did not vary much, or if they did, did not vary systematically; (c) was reading with some particular criterion in mind; and (d) read alone. Nothing can be revealed by such a design about subject, orienting task, materials, criterial task effects on text processing, or social factors influencing reactions to text, because there is no systematic variation of these factors in such designs. In studies where there was some systematic variation of a factor, the most likely one was a subject characteristic. As we discussed in the last chapter, subject manipulations, in fact, made a difference, where more experienced readers (and readers with considerable prior knowledge related to the reading task) were typically more constructively reactive than less experienced readers, at least with the outcome measures used to date. Although there were studies in which several different types of readings were processed (e.g., expositions vs. narratives; different types of short stories), typically only one or two examples of each text type was included in the study, making it difficult to know whether any differences in processing with respect to the pieces were due to the cited dimension of difference, some unacknowledged dimension of difference, or some idiosyncrasy of the particular pieces read.

This is a particularly regrettable situation because there are very good theoretical reasons to expect that constructive responsivity to text is going to vary tremendously depending on situational factors. For example, a point we made earlier was that when instructions included experimenter prompts to particular processes, the processes seemed to show up in protocols. The only way to know how certainly and how well readers modify their processing in reaction to situational pressures is to compare constructive responsivity with such pressures present against when they are absent, with other factors held constant. One very good possibility, consistent with Jenkin's (1979) analysis, is that whether such pressures alter processing depends on reader characteristics, reasons for reading, and the type of material being read. Thus, a child instructed to attempt to infer information not explicitly stated in text might attempt to do so regardless of the reading goal or type of material. An adult might only respond to the same inference instruction if the criterion task was demanding (e.g., recall, question answering) and if the materials were related to his or her prior knowledge, thus permitting ready inferences. Whether such a situational hypothesis is credible, however, is anyone's guess in the absence of systematic studies varying critical reader variables, orienting tasks, criterion tasks, and materials.

One reason we believe that the protocol analysts have not been more analytical in designing and planning studies to date is that, previously, much researcher effort was devoted to analyzing the data once it was obtained. Scoring has been a major hassle in these studies. Again, we believe that the systematic cataloging of the known conscious processes during reading should alleviate this difficulty for researchers and thus free up more resources that can be expended in pursuing interesting situational determinants of constructive responsivity, such as the ones Jenkins (1979) proposed interacted to determine cognitive activity in general.

VARIOUS AND SUNDRY RESEARCH DESIGN AND MEASUREMENT CHALLENGES AND CONCERNS

A variety of other methodological concerns also are apparent from study of the reading protocol investigations. Some of these are easily solvable, some are probably solvable with great effort, and others may prove insurmountable concerns. We review a few of the more prominent ones in this section.

Generation of Comparisons Between Different-Age, Different-Ability, Different-Anything Readers

There are already reports of different-age and different-ability level readers in the literature. The typical strategy has been for readers in these studies to read the same materials, with inferences about development of reading processes or differences in reading processes as a function of skill inferred from the differences in reported processes. There are many potential problems with such interpretations, however. For a variety of reasons, younger and less able readers would be expected to produce less complete verbal reports than older and more able readers (e.g., older and more able readers are more verbally skilled, with verbal skill an important determinant of at least the quality of self-reports; see Afflerbach & Johnston, 1984). Also, the same text is more difficult for younger and less able readers, so that the processes associated with difficult reading are collected for some participants and the processes associated with easy reading for other participants. Again, possible confounds created by the degree of automaticity of a reader processing text must be considered. Analogous confoundings occur with respect to other differences. Thus, if physics experts and novices read a text about physics, it is an easier reading task for the experts than the novices.

Solutions of some of these dilemmas have been proposed, but these also inevitably involve other confounds. Thus, Wyatt et al. (1993) had each of their social scientist participants select an article that was highly interesting to them. In doing so, reader interest across participants was held close to constant (i.e., all were reading an article that interested them, which was directly related to their area of expertise). In this case, readers and the specific articles read were confounded, with every reader processing a different article.

Confronting such concerns is not simply an exercise in methodological rigor, but also has a correspondingly high potential for advancing theory. For example, an important theoretical assumption is that the processes used when reading easy text are different (e.g., more automatic) than those used when reading challenging text (e.g., more deliberate). There is elegant work waiting to be done here—mapping out reported cognitive processes as a function of difficulty level for a wide range of ability levels. Is there a point with respect to low ability where a reader cannot read any text automatically? And what can readers do when they read such texts in an engaged manner? At the other extreme, is there a point where most reading is effortless, or where no texts require much effort? Of course, analogous speculations about processing could be offered with respect to age, interest, knowledge level, and other factors. This is just a specific aspect of the more general concern raised earlier in this chapter that reading processes as a function of subject characteristics are not well understood, especially as they interact with materials difference, orienting task differences, and variations in criterion.

Study of a Few Subjects Versus Large-*n* Investigations

Although some of the reading protocol analyses involved large numbers of participants, most were based on a relatively few participants. This largely reflects the costs of doing such research, with data collection, transcription, and analyses costs all very high. The difficulty with such an approach is that a great deal of confidence is put on the processes of a very few readers, despite the fact that, to the extent reading protocol researchers have looked (e.g., Lytle, 1982; Wade et al., 1990), tremendous differences in processes reported have been obtained, even when factors like ability level and age are held constant. That is, processing of a particular text is not reliable from reader to reader, one more reflection of the very great need to carefully analyze individual differences in text processing, a point made several times already in this chapter.

Our feeling is that such individual differences need to be confronted directly. In studies where they are not confronted, however, it seems unsafe to assume that the reports of a few subjects are representative of a population. Thus, when individual differences are generally going to be ignored, we prefer the traditional approach for dealing with unreliability in processes from person to person, which is to conduct large-n studies and document explicitly the within-sample differences in processes that occur. Because our assumption is that such individual differences could be explained, we also urge that the differences eventually be confronted and analyzed as a function of theoretically and pragmatically important differences between readers.

The set of categories generated in chapter 3 should do much to enable the conduct of many more large-n studies. Much effort has been devoted in previous work to the identification of sets of categories that can capture the data on hand. We are confident that most think-aloud process reports during reading would be classifiable with respect to the categories summarized in chapter 3, and thus believe that one expensive aspect of protocol analyses can be largely eliminated in future research efforts. Note as well that if we consider reader process reports in terms of the many categories in chapter 3, there is more opportunity than existed in the past to detect subtle differences in processing from reader to reader. Thus, the very real possibility exists that a much more sophisticated theory of individual differences during reading may emerge than if investigators continued to rely on scoring schemes not reflecting the full range of reader responses to text.

Transcriptions of Self-Report Data

Typically, before verbal protocols can be analyzed, they must be transcribed. Much is lost in such transcriptions, including many nonverbal nuances of meaning and meaning conveyed by tone of speech. Thus, a sarcastic reaction to a president's or senator's questionable ethics, "Well, that never happened when Dick Nixon was in the White House," might be completely misinterpreted if analyzed only on the basis of the words. In reading the existing protocols, no one could miss that readers' words were weighed more heavily than other means of expression they might have employed, although there were occasional references to nonverbal communciations and information conveyed by tone of voice. Attention to aspects of spoken language (including but not limited to speed and variability of speed of speaking, pauses, emphases, and intonation) will provide a more accurate account of what a reader spoke as a verbal reporter. There is a clear need for the development of transcription codes and symbols for preserving the quality of spoken language when it is transcribed. Our view is that every researcher collecting self-reports should assess whether he or she is losing nonverbal or tone-of-voice information that is important and take actions to make certain such information is represented in analyses of self-reports.

Sequences of Processes as the Unit of Analysis

Many theorists contend that readers coordinate their use of strategies. If that is true, the unit of analysis probably should not be the individual process, but rather sequences of processes. Although this possibility has been acknowledged since Afflerbach and Johnston (1984), we located no reports in which investigators reported sequences. From the vantage point of our new conceptual perspective, with its emphasis on constructive responsivity rather than strategic planning, there is not as much theoretical urgency in identifying sequences, if recurring sequences exist. For those investigators who continue to believe that planning before reading is the foremost determinant of strategic processing, rather than on-line responsivity, the search for sequences should be a high priority, for such sequences would provide considerable support for a high degree of planfulness in reading processes.

Identifying Situational Determinants of Processing

If constructive responsivity is to be taken seriously as a perspective, eventually it will be necessary to evaluate text (and other) situations to determine when particular processes are likely to occur, another challenge originally flagged by Afflerbach and Johnston (1984). Whether it is possible to do so reliably is anyone's guess at this point, for since the 1980s, there has not been systematic progress in establishing linkages between particular processes and text characteristics, orienting tasks, and criterion tasks. Of course, this is one more way of saying that the points of Jenkins tetrahedral model have been all but ignored in reading protocol analyses.

Short Readings as the Unit of Reading

Subjects in reading protocol studies invariably read fairly short texts, of which article-length pieces were the longest materials represented. Much of the time, the pieces read were much shorter, with paragraph-length readings not unusual. Of course, this was done in the interests of keeping studies managable. Voluminous think-aloud data can be generated even with respect to one paragraph. Still, this is not a very satisfactory state of affairs in a world in which people so often read material of varied length—from short articles to books. There definitely is a need for on-line study of reading processes when people read long pieces. We suspect that some type of sampling methods may need to be devised in order to tap such reading (e.g., every 20th page; a few minutes of reading at a time). We think that extremely interesting conceptual advances may come out of such research. Given the popularity over the years of works such as Adler and van Doren's (1972) *How to Read a Book*, we also infer that there is an audience for such information, many people who would like to know what skilled reading of longer pieces is really like. Were Adler and van Doren right? We do not know now, but we could probably find out using think-aloud and complementary methods.

Using Predetermined Categories Versus Developing One's Own Categories

Many investigators have invested tremendous efforts in developing categorizing schemes. Every one of these categorization schemes, however, is less extensive than the set of categorizations summarized in chapter 3. The decision to develop one's own categories should be made with the investment of effort in mind and with the knowledge that there now exists an extremely expansive set of categories (i.e., in chapter 3). We recognize that not every single distinction summarized in chapter 3 will prove reliably codable (at least not in every investigation), but also believe that it is a virtual certainty that an extremely extensive categorization system will remain if an investigator begins with the chapter 3 categories and simply collapses subcategories that prove impossible to discriminate from one another in the investigator's protocols. Of course, categories that simply do not occur in the investigator's sample can be eliminated as well. In short, although chapter 3 is not yet a well-developed scoring instrument, we believe it is a solid start that should permit rapid progress in identifying an exhaustive categorization scheme for coding reading protocols.

For researchers who are intent on constructing their own categories from scratch despite the existence of chapter 3, we believe that following Strauss and Corbin's (1990) approach to grounded theory generation is a dependable way of developing categorizations from data on hand (see Wyatt et al., 1993, for an example of how this was done). Essentially, a few raters search the data for dimensions, sorting data into tentative dimensions, with collapsing and realigning of dimensions continuing until there is consensus between raters and no new dimensions emerge. When an adequate model emerges (i.e., when the scoring scheme is saturated), no new classification distinctions should be needed to code data from new protocols. If new categories are needed, then the classification scheme is not yet complete. Consistent with Strauss and Corbin (1990), we believe that researchers should keep working at scoring scheme development until they reach the point where no changes in the scoring scheme are required to accommodate any of the data from new reading protocols.

CONCLUDING COMMENTS

We believe that the reading protocol studies provide a degree of detail that allows for some insights about several issues. Much of the work is important because it is explicit enough to permit the identification of many concerns. Such concerns flag that the extant data base is simply a start. We are encouraged that so much has been learned about reading, however, despite the limitations of work to date. We also view the present set of limitations as a set of arrows pointing the way to a more extensive science. There are many questions about conscious processes in reading that remain. We hope that the summary of conscious reading processes provided here, one that emanates from the reading protocol research to date, fuels enthusiasm for verbal protocol analysis as an approach to investigating reading. We also hope our efforts lead to more refined studies; we offered methodological recommendations in this chapter that would encourage further research in ways that would unambiguously also improve understanding of reading.

Rather than viewing this volume as a capstone summary of reading protocol analysis, we regard it more as a cornerstone. As is always the case in filling a cornerstone, we filled this volume with an organized set of information that would be informative to anyone who reads it in the future about the state of the world when the cornerstone was sealed. This book is a compendium of what can be learned from reading protocol studies now in existence. With this cornerstone in place, it is time to get busy developing a sound structure that will stretch a long way and rise high. If we make certain during this process that every new stone is as sturdy as the cornerstone, the ultimate structure will be very attractive and dependable; although every new stone will undoubtedly inspire the builders to build longer and higher. There is no end in sight with respect to reading protocol analyses, just a beginning that inspires new efforts that can be supported by the foundations presented here.

References

Adler, M. J., & van Doren, C. (1972). *How to read a book: The classic guide to intelligent reading.* New York: Simon & Schuster.

Afflerbach, P. (1990a). The influence of prior knowledge and text genre on readers' prediction strategies. *Journal of Reading Behavior, 22,* 131–148.

Afflerbach, P. (1990b). The influence of prior knowledge on expert readers' main idea construction strategies. *Reading Research Quarterly, 25,* 31–46.

Afflerbach, P., & Johnston, P. (1984). Research methodology: On the use of verbal reports in reading research. *Journal of Reading Behavior, 16,* 307–322.

Afflerbach, P., & Johnston, P. (1993). Eleven teachers composing language arts report cards: Conflicts in knowing and communicating. *Elementary School Journal, 94,* 73–86.

Anderson, J. R. (1983). *The architecture of cognition.* Cambridge MA: Harvard University Press.

Anderson, J. R. (1990). *Cognitive psychology and its implications.* San Francisco: Freeman.

Anderson, R. C., & Pearson, P. D. (1984). A schema-theoretic view of basic processes in reading. In P. D. Pearson (Ed.), *Handbook of reading research* (pp. 225–291). New York: Longman.

Baker, L. (1985). How do we know when we don't understand? Standards for evaluating text comprehension. In D. L. Forrest-Pressley, G. E. MacKinnon, & T. G. Waller (Eds.), *Metacognition, cognition, and human performance* (pp. 155–205). New York: Academic.

Baker, L. (1989). Metacognition, comprehension monitoring, and the adult reader. *Educational Psychology Review, 1,* 3–38.

Baker, L., & Brown, A. L. (1984). Metacognitive skills and reading. In P. D. Pearson, R. Barr, M. Kamil, & P. Mosenthal (Eds.), *Handbook of Reading Research* (pp. 353–394). New York: Longman.

Balota, D. A., d'Arcais, G. B. F., & Rayner, K. (Eds.) (1990). *Comprehension processes in reading.* Hillsdale NJ: Lawrence Erlbaum Associates.

Bartlett, F. C. (1932). *Remembering.* Cambridge, England: Cambridge University Press.

Bazerman, C. (1985). Physicists reading physics: Schema-laden purposes and purpose-laden schema. *Written Communication, 2,* 3–24.

Beach, R. W. (1972). *The literary response process of college students while reading and discussing three poems.* Doctoral dissertation, University of Illinois (*Dissertation Abstracts International* Order No. 73-17112).

Beach, R., & Hynds, S. (1991). Research on response to literature. In R. Barr, M. L. Kamil, P. B. Mosenthal, & P. D. Pearson (Eds.), *Handbook of reading research* (Vol. 2, pp. 453–489). New York: Longman.

Belenky, M., Clinchy, B., Goldberger, N., & Tarule, J. (1986). *Woman's ways of knowing: The development of self, voice, and mind.* New York: Basic Books.

Bereiter, C., & Bird, M. (1985). Use of thinking aloud in identification and teaching of reading comprehension strategies. *Cognition and Instruction, 2,* 131–156.

Bereiter, C., & Scardamalia, M. (1989). Intentional learning as a goal of instruction. In L. B. Resnick (Ed.), *Knowing, learning, and instruction: Essays in honor of Robert Glaser* (pp. 361–392). Hillsdale, NJ: Lawrence Erlbaum Associates.

Bereiter, C., & Scardamalia, M. (1993). *Surpassing ourselves: An inquiry into the nature and implications of expertise.* Chicago: Open Court.

Bloom, B. S. (1985). *Developing talent in young people.* New York: Ballantine.

Boring, E. (1953). A history of introspection. *Psychological Bulletin, 50,* 169–189.

Bridge, C., & Winograd, P. (1982). Readers' awareness of cohesive relationships during cloze comprehension. *Journal of Reading Behavior, 14,* 299–312.

Brown, A., & Day, J. (1983). Macrorules for summarizing strategies: The development of expertise. *Journal of Verbal Learning and Verbal Behavior, 22,* 1–14.

Brown, R., & Pressley, M. (1994). Self-regulated reading and getting meaning from text: The transactional strategies instruction model and its ongoing evaluation. In D. Schunk & B. Zimmerman (Eds.), *Self-regulation of learning and performance: Issues and educational applications* (pp. 155–179). Hillsdale, NJ: Lawrence Erlbaum Associates.

Bruce, B., & Rubin, A. (1984). Strategies for controlling hypothesis formation in reading. In J. Flood (Ed.), *Promoting reading comprehension* (pp. 97–112). Newark, DE: International Reading Association.

Bruner, J. S. (1973). *Beyond the information given.* New York: Norton.

Caron, T. A. (1989). Strategies for reading expository prose. In S. McCormick & J. Zutell (Eds.), *Cognitive and social perspectives for literacy research and instruction, 38th yearbook of the National Reading Conference* (pp. 293–300). Chicago: National Reading Conference.

Chan, C. K. K., Burtis, P. J., Scardamalia, M., & Bereiter, C. (1992). Constructive activity in learning from text. *American Educational Research Journal, 29,* 97–118.

Charney, D. (1993). A study in rhetorical reading: How evolutionists read "The Spaniards of San Marco." In J. Selzer (Eds.), *Understanding scientific prose.* Madison, WI: University of Wisconsin Press.

Chi, M. T. H., Glaser, R., & Farr, M. J. (1988). *The nature of expertise.* Hillsdale, NJ: Lawrence Erlbaum Associates.

Christopherson, S. L., Schultz, C. B., & Waern, Y. (1981). The effect of two contextual conditions on recall of a reading passage and on thought processes in reading. *Journal of Reading, 24,* 573–578.

Collins, A. M., Brown, J. S., & Larkin, K. M. (1980). Inferences in text understanding. In R. J. Spiro, B. C. Bruce, & W. F. Brewer (Eds.), *Theoretical issues in reading comprehension* (pp. 385–407). Hillsdale, NJ: Lawrence Erlbaum Associates.

Deegan, D. H. (1993, December). *Exploring the relations among reading strategies, comprehension, and performance in a specific domain: The case of law.* Paper presented at the annual meeting of the National Reading Conference, Charleston.

Deffner, G. (1988). Concurrent thinking aloud: An on-line tool for studying representations used in text understanding. *Text, 8,* 351–367.

de Groot, A. D. (1965). *Thought and choice in chess.* The Hague, Netherlands: Mouton.

de Groot, A. (1966). Perception and memory versus thought: Some old ideas and recent findings. In B. Kleinmuntz (Ed.), *Problem solving* (pp. 19–50). New York: Wiley.

Deshler, D. D., & Schumaker, J. R. (1988). An instructional model for teaching students how to learn. In J. L. Graden, J. E. Zins, & M. J. Curtis (Eds.), *Alternative educational delivery systems:*

Enhancing instructional outcomes for all students (pp. 391–411). Washington, DC: National Association of School Psychologists.

Driscoll, M. P. (1994). *Psychology of learning for instruction.* Boston: Allyn & Bacon.

Duncker, K. A. (1926). A qualitative (experimental and theoretical) study of productive thinking (solving of comprehensible problems). *Pedagogical Seminary, 33,* 642–708.

Duncker, K. A. (1945). On problem solving. *Psychological Monographs, 58,* 1–113 (Whole No. 270).

Earthman, E. A. (1989). *The lonely, quiet concert: Readers creating meaning from literary texts.* Unpublished doctoral dissertation, Stanford University, School of Education, Stanford.

Earthman, E. A. (1992). Creating the virtual work: Readers' processes in understanding literary texts. *Research in the Teaching of English, 26,* 351–384.

Eco, U. (1990). *The limits of interpretation.* Bloomington, IN: Indiana University Press.

El-Dinary, P. B., Pressley, M., Coy-Ogan, L., Schuder, T., & Strategies Instruction Teachers of Burnt Mills Elementary School (1994). *The teaching processes of transactional strategies instruction teachers as revealed through collaborative interviewing.* (Tech. Rep.). Albany, NY: State University of New York, Department of Educational Psychology and Statistics.

Ericsson, K. A. (1988). Concurrent verbal reports on text comprehension: A review. *Text, 8,* 295–325.

Ericsson, K. A., & Simon, H. A. (1984/1993). *Protocol analysis: Verbal reports as data.* Cambridge, MA: MIT Press. (Original work published 1983)

Fish, S. (1980). *Is there a text in this class? The authority of interpretive communities.* Cambridge, MA: Harvard University Press.

Flavell, J. H., Miller, S., & Miller, P. (1993). *Cognitive development* (3rd ed.). Englewood Cliffs, NJ: Prentice-Hall.

Fletcher, C. R. (1986). Strategies for the allocation of short-term memory during comprehension. *Journal of Memory and Language, 25,* 43–58.

Flower, L. (1987). Interpretive acts: Cognition and the construction of discourse. *Poetics, 16,* 109–130.

Garner, R., & Reis, R. (1981). Monitoring and resolving comprehension obstacles: An investigation of spontaneous lookbacks among upper-grade good and poor comprehenders. *Reading Research Quarterly, 16,* 569–582.

Gaskins, I. W., & Elliot, T. T. (1991). *Implementing cognitive strategy instruction across the school: The Benchmark manual for teachers.* Cambridge, MA: Brookline Books.

Geisler, C. (1991). Toward a sociocognitive model of literacy: Constructing mental models in philosophical conversation. In C. Bazerman & J. Paradis (Eds.), *Textual dynamics of the professions* (pp. 171–190). Madison: University of Wisconsin Press.

Glaser, R., & Chi, M. T. H. (1988). Introduction: What is it to be an expert? In M. T. H. Chi, R. Glaser, & M. J. Farr (Eds.), *The nature of expertise* (pp. xv–xxiix). Hillsdale, NJ: Lawrence Erlbaum Associates.

Glenberg, A. M., & Epstein, W. (1987). Inexpert calibration of comprehension. *Memory & Cognition, 15,* 84–93.

Goldman, S. R., & Saul, E. U. (1990). Flexibility in text processing: A strategy competition model. *Learning and Individual Differences, 2,* 181–219.

Graesser, A. C. (1993a). Introduction: Inference generation during text comprehension. *Discourse Processes, 16,* 1.

Graesser, A. C. (Ed.). (1993b). Inference generation during text comprehension [Special issue]. *Discourse Processes, 16*(1, 2).

Graesser, A. C., & Bower, G. H. (1990). *Inferences and text comprehension.* San Diego, CA: Academic Press.

Graesser, A. C., & Kreuz, R. J. (1993). A theory of inference generation during text comprehension. *Discourse Processes, 16,* 145–160.

Graves, B., & Frederiksen, C. H. (1991). Literary expertise in the description of fictional narrative. *Poetics, 20,* 1–26.

Grice, P. (1989). *Studies in the way of words.* Cambridge, MA: Harvard University Press.

Guthrie, J., Britten, T., & Barker, K. (1991). Roles of document structure, cognitive strategy, and awareness in searching for information. *Reading Research Quarterly, 26,* 300–324.

Haas, C., & Flower, L. (1988). Rhetorical reading strategies and the construction of meaning. *College Composition and Communication, 39,* 167–183.

Hare, V. C. (1981). Readers' problems identification and problem solving strategies for high- and low-knowledge articles. *Journal of Reading Behavior, 13,* 359–365.

Harris, K. R., & Pressley, M. (1991). The nature of cognitive strategy instruction: Interactive strategy construction. *Exceptional Children, 57,* 392–404.

Hayes, J. R. (1985). Three problems in teaching general skills. In S. F. Chipman, J. W. Segal, & R. Glaser (Eds.), *Thinking and learning skills: Vol. 2. Research and open questions* (pp. 391–405). Hillsdale, NJ: Lawrence Erlbaum Associates.

Holdaway, D. (1979). *The foundations of literacy.* Portsmouth, NH: Heineman.

Holland, N. (1975). *Five readers reading.* New Haven, CT: Yale University Press.

Huey, E. (1908). *The psychology and pedagogy of reading.* Cambridge, MA: MIT Press.

James, W. (1890). *The principles of psychology.* New York: Holt.

Jenkins, J. J. (1979). Four parts to remember: A tetrahedral model of memory experiments. In L. S. Cermak & F. I. M. Craik (Eds.), *Levels of processing in human memory* (pp. 429–446). Hillsdale, NJ: Lawrence Erlbaum Associates.

Johnston, P., & Afflerbach, P. (1985). The process of constructing main ideas from text. *Cognition and Instruction, 2,* 207–232.

Kavale, K., & Schreiner, R. (1979). The reading process of above average and average readers: A comparison of the use of reasoning strategies in responding to standardized comprehension measures. *Reading Research Quarterly, 15,* 102–128.

Kintgen, E. R. (1983). *The perception of poetry.* Bloomington: Indiana University Press.

Kintsch, W. (1988). The use of knowledge in discourse processing: A construction-integration model. *Psychological Review, 95,* 163–182.

Kintsch, W. (1993). Information accretion and reduction in text processing: Inferences. *Discourse Processes, 16,* 193–202.

Kletzien, S. B. (1991). Strategy use by good and poor comprehenders reading expository text of differing levels. *Reading Research Quarterly, 26,* 67–86.

Kletzien, S. B. (1992). Proficient and less proficient comprehenders' strategy use for different top-level structures. *Journal of Reading Behavior, 24,* 191–215.

Kucan, L. (1993, December). *Uncovering cognitive processes in reading.* Paper presented at the annual meeting of the National Reading Conference, Charleston.

Langer, E. J. (1989). *Mindfulness.* Reading, MA: Addison-Wesley.

Lesgold, A., Glaser, R., Rubinson, H., Klopfer, D., Feltovich, P., & Wang, Y. (1988). Expertise in a complex skill: Diagnosing x-ray pictures. In M. T. H. Chi, R. Glaser, & M. J. Farr (Eds.), *The nature of expertise* (pp. 311–342). Hillsdale, NJ: Lawrence Erlbaum Associates.

Levin, J. R., & Pressley, M. (1981). Improving childrens' prose comprehension: Selected strategies that seem to succeed. In C. M. Santa & B. L. Hayes (Eds.), *Children's prose comprehension: Research and practice* (pp. 44–71). Newark, DE: International Reading Association.

Long, D. L., & Golding, J. M. (1993). Superordinate goal inferences: Are they automatically generated during comprehension? *Discourse Processes, 16,* 55–74.

Long, D. L., Golding, J. M., & Graesser, A. C. (1992). A test of the on-line status of goal-related inferences. *Journal of Memory and Language, 31,* 634–647.

Lundeberg, M. A. (1987). Metacognitive aspects of reading comprehension: Studying understanding in legal case analysis. *Reading Research Quarterly, 22,* 407–432.

Lytle, S. L. (1982). *Exploring comprehension style: A study of twelfth-grade readers' transactions with texts.* Doctoral dissertation, University of Pennsylvania (University Microfilms No. 82-27292).

Magliano, J. P., & Graesser, A. C. (1993). A three-pronged method for studying inference generation in literary text. *Poetics, 20,* 193–232.

Marbe, K. (1901). *Experimentell-psychologische: Untersuchungen uber das Urteil.* Leipzig: Engelmann. (Reprinted and translated in J. Mandler & G. Mandler [Eds.]. [1964] *Thinking: From association to gestalt* [pp. 143–148]. New York: Wiley.)

Markman, E. M. (1977). Realizing that you don't understand: A preliminary investigation. *Child Development, 46,* 986–992.

Markman, E. M. (1981). Comprehension monitoring. In W. P. Dickson (Ed.), *Children's oral communication skills* (pp. 61–84). New York: Academic Press.

Mathison, S. (1988). Why triangulate? *Educational Researcher, 17*(2), 13–17.

McCallister, J. (1930). Reading difficulties in studying content subjects. *Elementary School Journal, 31,* 191–201.

Meyers, J., Lytle, S., Palladino, D., Devenpeck, G., & Green, M. (1990). Think-aloud protocol analysis: An investigation of reading comprehension strategies in fourth- and fifth-grade students. *Journal of Psychoeducational Assessment, 8,* 112–127.

Miller, G. A., Gallanter, E., & Pribram, K. H. (1960). *Plans and the structure of behavior.* New York: Holt, Rinehart & Winston.

Minsky, M. (1975). A framework for representing knowledge. In P. H. Winston (Ed.), *The psychology of computer vision* (pp. 211–277). New York: McGraw-Hill.

Moshman, D. (1982). Exogenous, endogenous, and dialectical constructivism. *Developmental Review, 2,* 372–384.

Nisbett, R. E., & Wilson, T. D. (1977). Telling more than we can know: Verbal reports on mental processes. *Psychological Review, 84,* 231–259.

Norris, S. P. (1990). Effect of eliciting verbal reports of thinking on critical thinking test performance. *Journal of Educational Measurement, 27,* 41–58.

Norris, S. P. (1992). A demonstration of the use of verbal reports of thinking in multiple-choice critical thinking test design. *Alberta Journal of Educational Research, 38,* 153–176.

Olshavsky, J. E. (1976–1977). Reading as problem solving: An investigation of strategies. *Reading Research Quarterly, 12,* 654–674.

Olson, G. M., Mack, R. L., & Duffy, S. A. (1981). Cognitive aspects of genre. *Poetics, 10,* 283–315.

Palincsar, A. S., & Brown, A. L. (1984). Reciprocal teaching of comprehension-fostering and monitoring activities. *Cognition and Instruction, 1,* 117–175.

Pearson, P. D., & Fielding, L. (1991). Comprehension instruction. In R. Barr, M. L. Kamil, P. B. Mosenthal, & P. D. Pearson (Eds.), *Handbook of reading research* (Vol. 2, pp. 815–860). New York: Longman.

Peterson, P., Swing, S., Braverman, M., & Buss, R. (1982). Students' aptitudes and their reports of cognitive processes during instruction. *Journal of Educational Psychology, 74,* 535–547.

Phillips, L. M. (1988). Young readers' inference strategies in reading comprehension. *Cognition and Instruction, 5,* 193–222.

Piekarz, J. (1954). *Individual responses in interpretive responses in reading.* Unpublished doctoral dissertation, University of Chicago.

Polya, G. (1954a). *Mathematics and plausible reasoning:* (a) *Induction and analogy in mathematics.* Princeton, NJ: Princeton University Press.

Polya, G. (1954b). *Patterns of plausible inference.* Princeton, NJ: Princeton University Press.

Poplin, M. S. (1988a). Holistic/constructivist principles of the teaching/learning process: Implications for the field of learning disabilities. *Journal of Learning Disabilities, 21,* 401–416.

Poplin, M. S. (1988b). The reductionistic fallacy in learning disabilities: Replicating the past by reducing the present. *Journal of Learning Disabilities, 21,* 389–400.

Pressley, M. (1994). Embracing complexity: Studying good information processing and how it might develop. *Learning and Individual Differences.*

Pressley, M., Borkowski, J. G., & Schneider, W. (1987). Cognitive strategies: Good strategy users coordinate meta-cognition and knowledge. In R. Vasta & G. Whitehurst (Eds.), *Annals of child development* (Vol. 4, pp. 89–129). Greenwich, CT: JAI.

Pressley, M., Borkowski, J. G., & Schneider, W. (1989). Good information processing: What it is and what education can do to promote it. *International Journal of Educational Research, 13,* 866–878.

Pressley, M., El-Dinary, P. B., Gaskins, I., Schuder, T., Bergman, J. L., Almasi, J., & Brown, R. (1992). Beyond direct explanation: Transactional instruction of reading comprehension strategies. *Elementary School Journal, 92,* 511–554.

Pressley, M., & Ghatala, E. S. (1990). Self-regulated learning: Monitoring learning from text. *Educational Psychologist, 25,* 19–34.

Pressley, M., Harris, K. R., & Marks, M. B. (1992). But good strategy instructors are constructivists!! *Educational Psychology Review, 4,* 1–32.

Pressley, M., Johnson, C. J., Symons, S., McGoldrick, J. A., & Kurita, J. A. (1989). Strategies that improve memory and comprehension of what is read. *Elementary School Journal, 90,* 3–32.

Pressley, M., & Levin, J. R. (1977). Developmental differences in subjects' associative learning strategies and performance: Assessing a hypothesis. *Journal of Experimental Child Psychology, 24,* 431–439.

Pressley, M., Levin, J. R., & Ghatala, E. S. (1988). Strategy-comparison opportunities promote long-term strategy use. *Contemporary Educational Psychology, 13,* 157–168.

Pressley, M. (with McCormick, C. B.). (1995). *Advanced educational psychology.* New York: Harper Collins.

Pressley, M., Wood, E., Woloshyn, V. E., Martin, V., King, A., & Menke, D. (1992). Encouraging mindful use of prior knowledge: Attempting to construct explanatory answers facilitates learning. *Educational Psychologist, 27,* 91–110.

Pritchard, R. (1990a). The effects of cultural schemata on reading processing strategies. *Reading Research Quarterly, 25,* 273–295.

Pritchard, R. (1990b). The evoluation of introspective methodology and its implications for studying the reading process. *Reading Psychology: An International Quarterly, 11,* 1–13.

Rauenbusch, F., & Bereiter, C. (1991). Making reading more difficult: A degraded text microworld for teaching reading comprehension strategies. *Cognition and Instruction, 8,* 181–206.

Richards, I. (1929). *Practical criticism.* New York: Harcourt, Brace, & World.

Rogers, T. (1991). Students as literary critics: The interpretive experiences, beliefs, and processes of ninth-grade students. *Journal of Reading Behavior, 23,* 391–423.

Rosenblatt, L. (1938). *Literature as exploration.* New York: Modern Language Association.

Rosenblatt, L. M. (1978). *The reader, the text, the poem: The transactional theory of the literary work.* Carbondale: Southern Illinois University Press.

Rosenshine, B., & Meister, C. (1992). *Reciprocal teaching: A review of nineteen experimental studies.* Manuscript submitted for publication, University of Illinois, Department of Educational Psychology, Champaign-Urbana.

Rumelhart, D., & Norman, D. (1975). The active structural network. In D. Norman, D. Rumelhart, & LNR Research Group (Eds.), *Explorations in cognition* (pp. 35–64). San Francisco: Freeman.

Rumelhart, D., & Norman, D. (1978). Accretion, tuning, and restructuring: Three modes of learning. In J. W. Cotton & R. L. Klatzky (Eds.), *Semantic factors in cognition* (pp. 37–53). Hillsdale, NJ: Lawrence Erlbaum Associates.

Saloman, G., & Globerson, T. (1987). Skill may not be enough: The role of mindfulness in learning and transfer. *International Journal of Educational Research, 11,* 623–637.

Samuels, S. J., & Kamil, M. L. (1984). Models of the reading process. In P. D. Pearson (Ed.), *Handbook of reading research* (pp. 185–224). New York: Longman.

Schank, R. C., & Abelson, R. P. (1977). *Scripts, plans, goals, and understanding.* Hillsdale, NJ: Lawrence Erlbaum Associates.

Schmalhofer, F., & Boschert, S. (1988). Differences in verbalization during knowledge acquisition from texts and discovery learning from example situations. *Text, 8,* 369–393.

Schwegler, R. A., & Shamoon, L. K. (1991). Meaning attribution in ambiguous texts in sociology. In C. Bazerman & J. Paradis (Eds.), *Textual dynamics of the professions* (pp. 216–233). Madison: University of Wisconsin Press.

Shearer, B., Coballes-Vega, C., & Lundeberg, M. (1993, December). *How do teachers who are professionally active select, read, and use professional journals?* Paper presented at the annual meeting of the National Reading Conference Charleston.

Simon, H. A., & Chase, W. G. (1973). Skill in chess. *American Scientist, 61*, 394–403.

Simon, D., & Simon, H. (1978). Individual differences in solving physics problems. In R. Siegler (Ed.), *Children's thinking: What develops?* (pp. 325–348). Hillsdale, NJ: Lawrence Erlbaum Associates.

Squire, J. R. (1964). *The responses of adolescents while reading four short stories*. Champaign, IL: National Council of Teachers of English.

Strang, R. (1970). *Learning to read—Insight for educators*. Toronto: OISE.

Strauss, A., & Corbin, J. (1990). *Basics of qualitative research: Grounded theory procedures and techniques*. Newbury Park, CA: Sage.

Titchener, E. B. (1912a). Prolegomena to a study of introspection. *American Journal of Psychology, 23*, 427–448.

Titchener, E. B. (1912b). The schema of introspection. *American Journal of Psychology, 23*, 485–508.

Trabasso, T., & Suh, S. (1993). Understanding text: Achieving explanatory coherence through on-line inferences and mental operations in working memory. *Discourse Processes, 16*, 3–34.

van den Broek, P. (1990a). Causal inferences and the comprehension of narrative texts. In A. C. Graesser & G. H. Bower (Eds.), *The psychology of learning and motivation: Vol. 25. Inferences and text comprehension* (pp. 197–212). San Diego, CA: Academic Press.

van den Broek, P. (1990b). The causal inference maker: Towards a process model of inference generation in text comprehension. In D. A. Balota, G. B. Flores d'Arcais, & K. Rayner (Eds.), *Comprehension processes in reading* (pp. 423–445). Hillsdale, NJ: Lawrence Erlbaum Associates.

van den Broek, P., Fletcher, C. R., & Risden, K. (1993). Investigations of inferential processes in reading: A theoretical and methodological integration. *Discourse Processes, 16*, 169–180.

van den Broek, P., & Lorch, R. F., Jr. (1993). Network representations of causal relations in memory for narrative texts: Evidence from primed recognition. *Discourse Processes, 16*, 75–98.

van Dijk, T. A., & Kintsch, W. (1983). *Strategies of discourse comprehension*. New York: Academic Press.

Wade, S. E., Trathen, W., & Schraw, G. (1990). An analysis of spontaneous study strategies. *Reading Research Quarterly, 25*, 147–166.

Waern, Y. (1988). Thoughts on text in context: Applying the think-aloud method to text processing. *Text, 8*, 327–350.

Watson, J. B. (1913). Psychology as the behaviorist views it. *Psychological Review, 20*, 158–177.

Watson, J. B. (1920). Is thinking merely the action of language mechanisms? *British Journal of Psychology, 11*, 87–104.

Weaver, C. A. III, & Kintsch, W. (1991). Expository text. In R. Barr, M. L. Kamil, P. B. Mosenthal, & P. D. Pearson (Eds.), *Handbook of reading research* (Vol. 2, pp. 230–245). New York: Longman.

Werner, H., & Kaplan, E. (1950). Development of word meaning through verbal context: An experimental study. *The Journal of Psychology, 29*, 251–257.

Williams, J. P. (1993). Comprehension of students with and without learning disabilities: Identification of narrative themes and idiosyncratic text representation. *Journal of Educational Psychology, 85*, 631–641.

Wineberg, S. S. (1991). On the reading of historical texts: Notes on the breach between school and academy. *American Educational Research Journal, 28*, 495–520.

Wong, B. Y. L., & Jones, W. (1982). Increasing metacomprehension in learning-disabled and normally achieving students through self-questioning training. *Learning Disabilities Quarterly, 5*, 228–240.

Wood, B., & Zakaluk, B. (1992, December). *The main ideas comprehension processing of teachers as expert readers*. Paper presented at the National Reading Conference, San Antonio.

Wyatt, D., Pressley, M., El-Dinary, P. B., Stein, S., Evans, P., & Brown, R. (1993). Reading behaviors of domain experts processing professional articles that are important to them: The critical role of worth and credibility monitoring. *Learning and Individual Differences, 5*, 49–72.

Author Index

Subject Index

→ Think about our own
reading processes as we
read through our issues

does S. read & think aloud
or only think aloud
while she reads to
herself?

begin w/ discussion of
constructive nature
of reading

interviews before and after each, reading task   10 minute

4 days.
2 text from school
reading list
2 mag of her choice

3 person protocol
Lauren - Annie - me.   recording
(asking   +
???)   talking notes

processes that
show progress
toward skilled
reading

maybe read one line at a time?
Lauren prompts her - red dot after
every line
2 par. at a time

note her body language

toward a skilled reading??